THE THEORY OF
ECONOMIC DEVELOPMENT
IN THE HISTORY OF
ECONOMIC THOUGHT

BEING THE CHICHELE LECTURES FOR 1966,
REVISED AND EXTENDED

Lionel Charles Robbins

LORD ROBBINS

MACMILLAN
LONDON · MELBOURNE · TORONTO
ST MARTIN'S PRESS
NEW YORK
1968

© Lord Robbins 1968

Published by
MACMILLAN AND CO LTD
Little Essex Street London W C 2
and also at Bombay Calcutta and Madras
Macmillan South Africa (Publishers) Pty Ltd Johannesburg
The Macmillan Company of Australia Pty Ltd Melbourne
The Macmillan Company of Canada Ltd Toronto
St Martin's Press Inc New York

Library of Congress catalog card no. 68-29378

Printed in Great Britain by
R. & R. CLARK, LTD., EDINBURGH

TO JOHN AND URSULA HICKS

WITH AFFECTION AND ADMIRATION

CONTENTS

Contents

FOREWORD

THIS book is the outcome of an invitation by the Warden and
Fellows of All Souls to deliver the Chichele Lectures for 1966.
The lectures as delivered were four in number. But since then I
have added three more in order to make the coverage more adequate.

My objective is very limited. I concentrate solely on the history
of the main propositions of the theory of development as they
would apply to a closed economy: I make no attempt to deal with
international trade or finance in this connection. Moreover, even
within this area, there is a further limitation. As I explain at some
length in the opening lecture, the propositions which I discuss
relate to the broad problem of why development takes place: they
do not deal with the more detailed problem of the exact path that
it may follow. To use technical jargon, I am concerned with the
comparative statics, rather than the dynamics, of the subject.

The reasons for this limitation are twofold. First the lectures
were on a foundation traditionally dedicated to history; and
dynamic theories of growth are essentially a contemporary development which to discuss in the requisite detail would have been
inappropriate in such a context. Secondly, while these developments are of great intellectual interest, at their present stage they
offer very little guidance for broad speculation concerning human
progress, still less for practical policy. The statical parts of the
theory, however, which are the main substance of the historical
discussions, while clearly limited in immediate applicability, have
a more obvious reference to reality. Moreover, in the excitement
of current speculation, it is possible that they may be neglected.
Keynes once remarked that he did 'not know which makes a man
more conservative, to know nothing but the present or nothing

but the past'. I do not think that contempory economic thought runs any danger whatever of the latter state of mind. But I confess that the suspicion has sometimes come into my head that, in certain quarters at least, there may be some slight risk of the former.

In thus presenting an historical essay, I should like to make it clear that it makes no pretension to completeness. It is essentially a selective discussion of famous propositions rather than an exhaustive study of the relevant literature; and it has no claim to originality other than that of arrangement and appraisal. It is a broad survey rather than a comprehensive history. I hope that my retention of the lecture-form may help to keep this in mind.

As in my other works on the history of economic thought, I have tried as far as possible to let the various authors dealt with speak for themselves rather than make them the subject of impressionistic description. This necessarily involves extensive quotation which those who wish to read quickly may find somewhat fatiguing. But I would claim at least for this method that, even if my interpretations and assessments are erroneous, it does provide a body of authentic information on which the reflective reader may form an independent judgment.

I would like to take this opportunity of thanking my hosts at All Souls both for the honour which they did me by their invitation and for their generous hospitality during the weeks when the lectures were being delivered.

ROBBINS

London School of Economics
      December 1967

GENERAL VIEW

I. INTRODUCTORY

THE subject of these lectures is the Theory of Economic Development. But, as befits the foundation under which they are delivered, their object is historical rather than analytical. My intention is to trace the evolution of ideas on this subject rather than to contribute to contemporary speculation. My full title therefore is *not* The Theory of Economic Development in Modern Economic Analysis, but rather The Theory of Economic Development in the History of Economic Thought.

This distinction of focus happens to coincide, more or less, with an analytical distinction. For the theory of economic development addresses itself to two types of question. It asks what are the fundamental causes or conditions of economic development and it asks what path development will take, given any particular configuration of these factors or fundamental conditions. If you like to put things this way, we can say that it asks *why* questions and *how* questions: it asks why development takes place and how it happens. We must not make the distinction too sharp. Obviously there is an area in which the two types of question shade into one another; and perhaps in the end the answers should be part of a unified theory. But the broad contrast is clear enough and corresponds to differences in the literature of the subject.

In recent years the emphasis has tended to be chiefly on the *how* questions. A substantial proportion of current work in this field consists in the analysis of the actual process of development as exhibited in various abstract models. This type of inquiry has already produced one masterpiece, Sir John Hicks' *Growth and*

Capital. But for the most part, it is still in a very inchoate state: and the extent to which it can be used either as a guide to practice or as an interpretation of history is very slender.

In the earlier literature the position is different. There the emphasis is definitely on the *why* questions — the questions relating to the fundamental conditions of development — and, although it would be wrong to claim that even now the theory of the subject is complete, there is a substantial body of generalisations which seem to have some bearing both on present problems and past experience. At any rate, it is this field that I shall be exploring — the evolution of ideas concerning the basic causes of economic growth and decline. The history, as distinct from the analysis, of theories of the path is so brief that it is not yet appropriate for this sort of treatment.

There are, however, in the historical literature two manifestations of what may perhaps be regarded as *how* theories which, because I shall not be including them in this survey, deserve mention at this stage.

The first is a certain aspect of Marxian theory. I do not think it is to be denied that there is what may be called a *how* theory of development in the broader implications of Marxian analysis. The theory of progressive impoverishment, of the increasing severity of crises, of the intensification of class war and of the final Messianic explosion in which the integument of capitalist society is disrupted and the expropriators are expropriated, is certainly, in a sense, a theory of development — even if the developments described may not necessarily be viewed as tending in an upward sense by all the parties concerned. But it is a type of theory which clearly involves psychological and sociological assumptions not usually regarded as part and parcel of economics strictly so-called. And since the results are so palpably out of harmony with the facts of development since Marx wrote, it seems legitimate to leave it out of this limited survey.

The other kind of theory which I do not intend to discuss, but which might by some be regarded as dealing with *how* questions, is that which the Germans call stage-theory. Economic development is conceived as taking place in different stages, the hunting economy, the agrarian economy, the commercial economy, the industrial economy and so on; and each ideal type is supposed to have salient characteristics which it is the main business of this kind of theory to describe. I will not deny that if this sort of thing is well written up it has entertaining qualities, valuable perhaps in after-dinner conversation. But I confess that, for me, the greater part of it is very sterile, neither good history nor significant theory. In my judgment it is no accident that much of the effort of economic historians in the last few decades has had to be devoted to the debunking of stage-theory as a guide to what has actually happened. And, although at first sight it may seem to be a theory of *how* development takes place, on closer inspection it proves merely to be an account of how it is thought past history has taken place; it is a description of results rather than causes. So far as I can see, it carries with it little predictive power, nor does it explain even the past in terms which marry easily with any accepted categories of pure theory. I make no apology therefore for leaving it out altogether.[1]

My treatment will fall into three parts. In this, my first lecture, I shall try to give a general view of the subject. Then successively in the next five lectures I shall discuss the role in economic development of the number of the population, of accumulation, of education and technical knowledge, of organisation and of money. Finally I shall conclude with some appraisal of historic attitudes to the desirability of development.

2. THE DEFINITION OF ECONOMIC DEVELOPMENT

Before setting out on these inquiries, I ought perhaps to state explicitly what I intend to mean by development. This is a term which quite obviously is capable of a variety of meanings. In

[1] For a powerful critique of stage-theory, see Walter Eucken, *Die Grundlagen der Nationalökonomie* (1947), especially pp. 63–111.

regard to economic systems it might mean increase in the absolute size of, for instance, capital or annual production regardless of the size of the population — the sense in which it was commonly used before the rise of classical economics and in which it is sometimes used in popular discussion today. It might mean increase in complexity, in the articulation of various different functions. It might mean progress towards some ethically defined goal. But I shall not use this term in any of these senses. The sense in which I shall use it throughout will be the sense in which it is used nowadays in the various comparative tables to which we have recourse when we discuss degrees of development, and the sense in which, since the days of Adam Smith's *The Wealth of Nations*, it has been used in the so-called theory of production. That is to say, I shall use it in relation to movements in real income per head and to potential in this respect — real income being conceived as a stream of availability of goods and services as distinct from the experiences or satisfactions to which it gives rise. In doing this, I am not at all unaware of the very considerable conceptual difficulties involved in measurements of this kind; if need be I could at once elaborate a whole series of methodological scruples and reservations. But my main business here is to give an account of an evolution of thought; and at this stage I think that we can defer considerations of this sort and proceed with the good sense of the historical perspective.

If we take the term development in this sense, it is surprising what a considerable extent of the economic thought of the past can be brought into the picture. Needless to say, it would be absurd to claim that the whole corpus can be so classified. The fundamental theories of structural relationships, the theories of value and distribution, for instance, can be studied, as in modern equilibrium analysis, quite independently of the idea of development. Yet if we realise that development conceived algebraically — i.e. with either a plus or a minus sign, is more or less the same as change on an aggregate or near-aggregate scale, and if we realise the underlying normative urge of much of the speculation of the past, it is not difficult to see what a large part of the field may be regarded as relevant. The search for causes of improvement of production per head informs a great deal of the literature of the subject. It is the object of this lecture to demonstrate this in some detail.

3. ECONOMIC DEVELOPMENT IN THE LITERATURE OF MERCANTILISM

I begin with the literature of mercantilism. This term derives from Adam Smith who depicted what he called the mercantile theory of wealth as preoccupied with policies designed to produce a favourable balance of trade; and if we take it in this sense, I do not think there is much to be said for associating it directly with the idea of development. It is still a matter of controversy why this particular objective was chosen. Was it because importance was attached to the accumulation of the precious metals *per se* or as a reserve against future contingencies? Or was it because of a perception, inadequately explained, of the easement to credit and employment prevailing when the balance was favourable? There is certainly more to be said for the latter hypothesis than the nineteenth-century classical economists were prepared to recognise. But it would be difficult to find any advocacy of a favourable balance which specifically made it a prerequisite of development. Rather the contrary indeed: the development of particular industries was justified in terms of their favourable effects on the balance.

If, however, we use the term mercantilism in the wider sense in which it has been used by Schmoller and his school and — with much greater distinction — by Eli Heckscher, if, that is to say, we use it to cover most of the economic literature in the period between the end of the Middle Ages and the coming of classical economics,[1] then there is certainly much to be found which bears upon our subject even though it is aggregate production rather than production per head which usually seems the object of

[1] Including what the Germans call Kameralism.

discussion. For the *raison d'être* of this literature, when it was not merely the pursuit of special interests, was essentially national policy, nation-building if you like to put it pretentiously; and although this had many aspects other than economic development, yet a great deal of it could quite reasonably be included under the heading.

It would be difficult to claim, however, that from the point of view of these lectures, this literature, vast as it is, offers very much of general interest. The almost endless flood of pamphlets advocating the development of this or that form of economic activity — the fisheries, the woollen industry, shipping, the draining of fens, the creation of roads and waterways — were doubtless often meritorious enough in their historical setting and have interest too in that context.[1] But of general significance for the theory of economic development, there is little of any value. Presumably some case can be made for the view that the argument for the protection of infant industries has its antecedents here[2] — there are certainly plenty of arguments for protection of one kind or another. But for the most part, you have to have quite a special kind of enthusiasm to read back into this mass of *ad hoc* suggestions and improvisations anything which deserves the name of general theory.

4.   PHYSIOCRACY AS A THEORY OF DEVELOPMENT

For the real beginnings of such a theory, as you might expect, we have to look to the literature of the eighteenth century when the speculative intellect, stimulated by the discoveries of natural science, began to consider the economic phenomena of society as a whole and to make general statements about their causal relationships. It is in the eighteenth century that economics emerges as

[1] A typical example is Andrew Yarranton's somewhat neglected *England's Improvement By Sea and Land* (1677).

[2] See Lecture V, section 9, p. 112 *seq*.

a systematic body of thought and it is in the eighteenth century that we find the beginnings of attention to the most general causes of development.

If I were asked to pick out one single work which most typifies the appearance in the eighteenth century of scientific economics, I should have no hesitation in citing Cantillon's *Essai sur la Nature du Commerce*, which with its system and objectivity, its deep analytical insight and its wide empirical knowledge is almost unique in that or any later age. But in spite of many penetrating *obiter dicta* on the subject, I should not cite it as being especially concerned with the theory of development. Cantillon was at once too detached from policy and too interested in unveiling the essential interconnections of the system of production and exchange to put development as such in the foreground of his analysis. For that we have to look to the works of the Physiocrats and to Adam Smith's *Wealth of Nations*.

To begin with the Physiocrats. There can be no shadow of doubt that their focus was upon development. More than most, the Physiocratic literature is encumbered by a superstructure of what Comte would have called metaphysics — natural law and the infallible method whereby societies may be happy and just. But at the core is a theory of development. Quesnay and his disciples saw the French economy burdened with a load of regulations which they regarded as inimical to productivity, and their analysis was directed to show why this was so and how the removal of these regulations would lead to greater prosperity.

Unfortunately this analysis was vitiated by an important technical error, the restriction of the idea of productive labour to agricultural and extractive industry — outside these groups, all labour engaged in manufacture, transport, commerce and finance was *ipso facto* unproductive or sterile. Now it is important to realise the nature of this error. They did not deny the *usefulness* of the unproductive labour; although the terminology was affectively toned, the division was analytical not pejorative.[1] But they did

[1] See, e.g., Baudeau, *Première Introduction à la Philosophie Économique*, ed. Dubois (Paris, 1910) p. 4: 'Les arts non productifs, bien

hold that, regardless of demand or the durability of the product, there was something essentially different between the labour which cut the wood in the forest and the labour which fashioned it into various commodities. And this was not just a matter of the mere use of words: it involved a conception which obscures rather than elucidates the nature of wealth and of the wealth-creating process.

Nevertheless, there was more in the Physiocratic system than this analytical ineptitude. The celebrated *Tableau Économique* of Quesnay was not, as its adepts contended, an invention which was on a par with the invention of writing or money. But it was a serious attempt to elucidate the circulation of wealth as defined in their system; in this respect it has some ancestral relationship to modern input–output analysis. And — what is more relevant to my theme — in Quesnay's *Premier Problème Économique*, in Mirabeau's *L'Ami des Hommes* and in the jointly written *Philosophie Rurale* of the two authors, it was overtly used to explain the mechanism of advance or decline, according as the prescriptions of the school were, or were not, adopted. I do not think that this aspect of the *Tableau* had much influence on subsequent thought, save perhaps on Marx's somewhat tortuous but nevertheless interesting reproduction tables. But in any just view of the history of the theory of development in the sense in which I am treating it, it certainly deserves honourable mention.[1]

loin d'être inutiles, font dans les états polices le charme et le soutien de la vie, la conservation et le bien-être de l'espèce humaine. . . . Ce n'est donc pour déprécier ou aviler cette espèce d'industrie très utile, très nécessaire, qu'il faut distinguer l'art fécond ou productif de l'art stérile ou non-productif. C'est qu'en effet l'un prépare et augmente la fécondité de la nature et de ses productions, l'autre se contente d'en profiter.'

[1] On the significance of the *Tableau* in this connection Professor R. L. Meek, *Economics of Physiocracy* (1962), should be consulted, especially pp. 287–96.

5. THE WEALTH OF NATIONS

The main credit for putting economic development on the map as a subject for general analysis belongs undoubtedly to Adam Smith. *The Wealth of Nations* is one of the great seminal works of world literature and as such has many aspects, as social philosophy, as economic history as well as political economy. And as political economy its coverage is wide, ranging from an exhibition of the essential structural relationships of an exchange economy practising division of labour, to the economic functions of the state and the canons of taxation. But, as the title itself implies, the central focus is on development — what makes the wealth of nations greater or less. It may be true, as some commentators have urged, that in the last analysis, Smith's prescriptions regarding policy were inspired as much by a concern for justice as by concern for the increase of riches. But whatever the ultimate verdict here, there can be no doubt that the main preoccupation of this book was that which is indicated by its title.

This emerges clearly at the outset where, in what he calls the 'Introduction and Plan of the Work', Smith sets forth his intentions and their rationale. For the first time in the history of economic thought, production per head, as distinct from aggregate production, is adopted as the central criterion: 'According . . ., as this produce, or what is purchased with it, bears a greater or smaller proportion to the number of those who are to consume it, the nations will be better or worse supplied with all the necessaries and conveniences for which it has occasion'.[1] And two main 'circumstances' are said to regulate this proportion: 'first . . . the skill, dexterity and judgement with which . . . labour is generally applied; and, secondly, by the proportion between the number of those who are employed in useful labour and that of those who are not so employed'. He then goes on to explain that the first two books — which constitute the analytical part of the work —

[1] Adam Smith, *The Wealth of Nations*, ed. Cannan (1904) vol. i, p. 1. All further references to *The Wealth of Nations* are to this edition.

are to be devoted to discussing respectively 'the causes of . . . improvement in the productive powers of labour' and the accumulation of capital.

This indeed is the true perspective of what follows. Admittedly much else comes in. In book I there is also a theory of value and distribution, in book II a theory of money and credit; and such is the importance of the treatment that these sections seem to acquire, as it were, autonomous existence. But this is to get them out of proportion. The theory of value and distribution, important as it is, is developed in order to show how the division of labour is organised in an exchange economy through the market for goods and services.[1] The theory of money and credit is part of a discussion of the nature of capital, preliminary to the analysis of accumulation. And in books III and IV, which deal respectively with 'the different Progress of Opulence in different Nations' and 'Systems of political Economy', the focus is still on development, either on what has actually occurred or on the beneficial or adverse effects of different theories of policy. Only in book V, 'Of the Revenue of the Sovereign or Commonwealth', do the criteria become more various. But even here the effect of policy upon productive efficiency occupies a large part of the picture. If the entire work were to be renamed The Theory and Practice of Economic Development, we should lose the felicity and the multiple implications of the actual title; but we should not do injustice to its main intentions.

6.   NINETEENTH-CENTURY CLASSICAL ECONOMICS

When we turn to the nineteenth-century classical economists, the picture is not so simple. The tendency, noticeable already in *The Wealth of Nations*, for the treatment of such subjects as value

---

[1] As is well known, there is no systematic treatment of distribution in the *Lectures on Justice, Police, Revenue and Arms*, ed. Cannan (1896), which are to be regarded, in the last three sections, as a first outline of the theory of *The Wealth of Nations*.

and distribution to detach themselves from the theory of productive organisation and to assume an autonomy of their own, had gathered strength. J. B. Say in his development of the Smithian system imposed a 'logical' division into Production, Distribution and Consumption. James Mill went one further and treated of Production, Distribution, Interchange and Consumption. It would be plainly wrong to suppose that the treatment under these headings was all focused upon the causes which make production per head greater or less. Ricardo was indeed exceptional in believing that the determination of the laws regulating distribution was 'the principle problem in Political Economy'[1] and that inquiry into the nature and causes of wealth was 'vain and delusive'.[2] But he was not exceptional in treating this and other

---

[1] David Ricardo, *Works*, ed. Sraffa (1951–2) vol. i, p. 5. All further references to Ricardo's *Works* are to this edition.

[2] Letter to Malthus, 9 October 1820, Ricardo, *Works*, vol. viii, p. 278. The whole passage is worth quotation: 'Political Economy you think is an enquiry into the nature of causes of wealth — I think it should rather be called an enquiry into the laws which determine the division of the produce of industry among the classes who concur in its formation. No law can be laid down respecting quantity, but a tolerably correct one can be laid down respecting proportions. Every day I am more satisfied that the former enquiry is vain and delusive, and the latter only the true objects of the science.' Against this, however, may be quoted a letter of 28 September 1821 (ibid., vol. ix, p. 83) in which he says: 'the great enquiries on which to fix our attention are the rise or fall of corn, labour, and commodities in real value. . . . It may be curious to develop the effect of an alteration of real value on money price, but mankind are only really interested in making labour productive, in the enjoyment of abundance, and in a good distribution of the produce obtained by capital and industry.' I think this should make it clear that the earlier somewhat drastic repudiation was simply a matter of determining an area in which something like precision was possible — an attitude with which anyone nurtured on the approach of the subjective theory of value can easily sympathise, even if in the last analysis he must agree not to condone. I speak as one who has sinned somewhat in this way myself at times. See Professor H. Myint's very justified strictures in the opening section of his valuable *Theories of Welfare Economics* (1948).

subjects as having interest in themselves regardless of their bearing on economic development.

Nevertheless it would be equally wrong to suppose that discussion of the influences making for growth dropped out of the picture. The sections dealing with production are essentially discussions of what makes production per head greater or less: and in this connection there are deployed most of the famous theorems derived from Adam Smith regarding division of labour and accumulation, plus the equally famous theorems derived from Malthus and the Corn Law controversy regarding the tendencies of population increase and diminishing returns in agriculture. Of Nassau Senior's 'Four Elementary Propositions of the Science', no less than three have this orientation. Moreover it must not be forgotten that, even under the heading distribution, a substantial part of the discussion relates to the *effects* — as distinct from the *causes* — of development.

All this comes out very clearly if we turn to the *Principles of Political Economy* of John Stuart Mill, which, avowedly, endeavoured to provide 'a work similar in its object and general conception to that of Adam Smith, but adapted to the more extended knowledge and improved ideas of the present age'.[1] It would be a mistake to let Mill's statement of intent lead one to expect a sharp concentration of the whole treatise on the causes of development: the plan with its various divisions is much more comprehensive than that. But it would be impossible to make the most superficial inspection of the contents table of book 1 on production, with its inquiries concerning the degrees of productiveness of productive agents at different times and different places and its treatment of the functions of capital and the combination (i.e. division) of labour, without realising that there is here attempted a systematic answer to all the main *why* questions of the theory of development. It is true that Mill, unlike his predecessors, disavowed fear of the coming of a stationary state. But

[1] John Stuart Mill, *Principles of Political Economy*, ed. Robson (1965) p. xcii. All further references to *Principles of Political Economy* are to this Toronto edition.

this does not mean that he was not profoundly interested in development. As we shall see in more detail later on in these lectures, the stationary state which he did not fear was not that which cast its shadow over the speculations of Smith or Ricardo. It was a stationary state in which a high level of development had been achieved by technical progress and accumulation and which was held at that level by restraint of population growth. It should be clear — to us if not to Mill himself — that a good deal of development would be needed, not only in Mill's day but also in our own, to reach this happy condition; and no one who takes the trouble to read Mill's book can doubt that one of its main underlying practical objectives was to provide prescriptions to that end.

The preoccupation of the classical writers with this problem is nowhere better illustrated than in the introduction to the *Outlines of Social Economy*, a work of popularisation by William Ellis, the friend and collaborator of John Stuart Mill and the founder of numerous schools. He opens with vivid contrasts between the wealth of the original inhabitants of Australia and North America and that of the contemporary societies in those countries. He paints in glowing colours the change in conditions in this country 'where twenty million now live in peace and security', where originally 'two millions only did live in strife and confusion'. And then he goes on to say that: 'History teaches us that the progress which we have made from barbarism to our actual state of civilisation has been gradual, although more rapid of late years than formerly; and reflection convinces us that there is ample room for further progress. It is our duty, then, since we are born into a world greatly improved by the exertions of our fathers, to hand it down still more improved to those who are to come after us. To perform this duty, the wish alone will not suffice; we must acquire knowledge to guide us in its performance. To know how to advance in civilisation or happiness, we ought to have a clear understanding of the causes of the progress already made and of the obstacles which retard our fathers' progress; and to this end we will at once direct our thoughts.'[1]

[1] William Ellis, *Outlines of Social Economy* (1846) pp. 1–4.

7. THE MARGINAL REVOLUTION

I now come to the seventies and the so-called Marginal Revolution which marks the full-scale beginning of modern economic analysis. It is, of course, an error to over-emphasise the element of revolution here. The sense of moving into a totally new world which pervades the contributions of Jevons, Walras and the Austrians, was to some extent a delusion. We can now see, as only Marshall saw at the time, a much greater degree of continuity in the evolution of thought than was perceived by these thinkers. Nevertheless there were real innovations here, innovations which changed the look and to some extent the emphasis of the whole corpus of economic theory.

Speaking broadly, I would say that the changes were twofold. First there was the greatly increased role of demand — demand for products, demand for productive services — which was the ultimate outcome of the reconciliation of the ideas of utility and value: this, with different degrees of emphasis, is the common element in all the contributions to this movement. Secondly, there is the perception and the analytical exhibition of the interdependence of all the factors in an economic universe: this is particularly the contribution of Walras with his equations of general economic equilibrium and — although with very different analytical intentions and much greater reserve concerning the applicability of such abstract constructions — of Marshall. Whatever the element of continuity in the ultimate historic picture, there can be no doubt that these two developments involved a notable change of emphasis.

From the point of view of this survey, this change manifested itself in a tendency to concentrate attention on allocation rather than development.[1] The economic problem was conceived as a problem of the disposition of *given* resources; and although this clearly involved the problem of choices between present and future,

[1] For an illuminating discussion of the contrast, see the work by Professor Myint cited above, especially ch. 1.

between consumption and accumulation, yet analysis tended to concentrate upon the conditions of achievement, or falling short, of various optima, rather than on the conditions of power to achieve optima of increasing range. For reasons which are pretty obvious, since they spring from real conceptual difficulties, there was less discussion of the movements of aggregates of production and the consequential averages, more of the movements of particular lines of production within given sets of constraints. It is no accident that, outside the theory of money, the discussion of practical questions in this early modern period relates much more to market forms, impediments to mobility, obstacles to trade, much less to the fundamental conditions of progress than in the classical period.

It is important not to make the contrast too sharp. For the most part, in so far as they did not relate to value and distribution, the earlier propositions were not repudiated, even if they were often ignored. Indeed they were frequently reproduced, if in rather a dead way, in the general textbooks of the period: and of course there were some economists of secondary influence who continued to follow the classical tradition. But I do not think it is open to question that the liveliness of research and speculation lay in the directions I have indicated, rather than in the theory of development. The lay reader of the *Economics of Welfare*, for instance, would be far more likely to be interested in divergences between private and social net product or degrees of monopoly than in questions of accumulation and decumulation and the development of the division of labour. And if this was true of Pigou's *magnum opus* how much truer was it of the products of the School of Lausanne or of first-generation Vienna.

8. MARSHALL AND SCHUMPETER

There are two conspicuous exceptions to the tendency I have been discussing, Alfred Marshall and Joseph Schumpeter.

I will speak first of Schumpeter, since he springs quite directly from the schools which otherwise display this tendency. His first book, the *Wesen und Hauptinhalt der theoretischen National-ökonomie*, which I fancy is seldom read today, is a highly individual amalgam of Viennese terminology and Walrasian analysis, more severally statical than it is easy to conceive in a work of such extensive dimensions and explicitly not concerned with problems of development. But this was followed by a work, equally theoretical, which was entirely concentrated on the nature and causes of development as such — the famous *Theorie der wirtschaftlichen Entwicklung*.

The argument of this work is highly individual. The essence of economic development is conceived as the rupture of existing patterns of economic relationships — the normal circular flow of statical analysis. And the agent of change is the path-breaking entrepreneur who, aided by the elasticity of the cash and credit system, is able at discontinuous intervals to wrest control of productive factors from their normal uses and reassemble them in novel combinations. Emulation brings in imitators and, for a time, the expansion of credit enables the upward surge to be sustained. Eventually, however, the movement exhausts itself. Depression then eliminates the unsound positions which have been adopted, leaving the economy purged and prepared for another wave of heroic innovation. We have thus a picture of both progress and fluctuation — a theory of development which is also a theory of the trade cycle, as conceived in the light of pre-1914 statistics. In spite of its highly sensational theme and what, to my way of thinking, is an essentially misleading theory of interest, it is certainly one of the outstand ingworks of the first quarter of this century and, like so much of Schumpeter's work, significantly thought-provoking even when it seems most perverse.

In sharp contrast to these somewhat hectic perspectives is the position of Alfred Marshall. As some of you may recollect, the motto of his great *Principles of Economics* is *Natura non facit saltum*; and, in the preface to the eighth edition, he goes out of his way to emphasise its moral: 'Economic evolution is gradual.

Its progress is sometimes arrested or reversed by political catas-
trophes: but its forward movements are never sudden; for even
in the Western World and Japan, it is based on habit, partly conscious, partly unconscious. And though an inventor, or an
organizer, or a financier of genius may seem to have modified the
economic structure of a people almost at a stroke; yet that part
of his influence, which has not been merely superficial and transitory, is found on inquiry to have done little more than bring to a
head a broad constructive movement which had long been in
preparation.'

Nevertheless Marshall's focus was upon growth. It is true that
he had discovered, either independently by himself or with the
aid of earlier mathematical economists — Cournot, Dupuit, von
Thünen — most of the celebrated innovations of the Marginal
Revolution — marginal utility, marginal productivity, the general
interdependence of economic quantities. But the use he made of
them was different. Unlike most of his contemporaries, he refused,
rightly or wrongly, to be tied down by the assumptions of statical
equilibrium. He employed what he called the statical method;
but it was in the interests of the study of change and growth. In
a famous letter to J. B. Clark, the author of a celebrated dichotomy
between the contents of static and dynamic analysis, he protested
that he 'could no more write one book about my static state and
another about my dynamic state, than I could write one book
about a yacht moving three miles an hour through the water which
was running against it, and another about a yacht moving through
the still water at five miles an hour.'[1] And in the preface from
which I have already quoted, while stating that 'the Mecca of the
economist lies in economic biology rather than economic dynamics',
he goes out of his way to insist that, even in dealing with foundations, as in the *Principles*, 'the keynote is that of dynamics rather
than statics'.

Hence, for all the modernity of its analytical apparatus, the preoccupation of Marshall's *Principles* is much more akin to that of the
earlier nineteenth-century economists than that of most of his

[1] *Memorials of Alfred Marshall*, ed. Pigou (1925) p. 415.

contemporaries; and it is this, quite as much as his retention of older conceptions of real costs or elasticity of the supply functions of productive services, which perhaps justifies the label 'neo-classical' which is often applied to his work. It is no accident that books v and vi of his great book, which deal respectively with Value and Distribution, should be preceded, as in the classical tradition, by book iv which treats of the Agents of Production and causes of variations in their efficiency.

9. TRADE CYCLE THEORY AND GROWTH

It is now time to look in directions other than the matrix of classical production theory and developments springing therefrom. For the modern treatment of economic development embraces some modes of analysis having a substantially different origin.

In this connection we may begin with the theory of the Trade Cycle. This theory, whatever other characteristics it may have, is certainly concerned with the ups and downs of output, either in the aggregate or at least over substantial parts of the field. It follows therefore that, though its immediate sphere of attention may be different, it is fundamentally concerned with movements some of which have a family resemblance to the movements of general development. Indeed it is possible to contend that these ups and downs are part of the mechanism of growth — or that growth would not be so rapid without them. As we have seen, this was the case argued in Schumpeter's famous essay. It was also the position tentatively adopted from time to time by no less an authority than the late Dennis Robertson.

But the connection between the two lines of speculation can be even more intimate than this. Since its first beginnings in the middle of the nineteenth century, the theory of the Trade Cycle has assumed many forms, from the sun-spot theory of Jevons to the theory of the propagation of random shocks of Wicksell and of Ragnar Frisch. But it has developed against a background of

actual growth; and it has gradually come to be realised that it is
at least probable that its most prominent characteristics are in
some way or other a product of the fact of growth — not merely
that growth may be *promoted* by cyclical variations, as in the
Schumpeter–Robertson constructions, but that, more fundamentally, the cycle may be *due* to something at work among the
factors causing growth. It is not necessary that this should be so.
One can imagine a cycle within a more or less stationary state —
caused perhaps by regularly recurring influences on the weather,
or even by some inherent tendency of the data to oscillate round
a fixed point rather than reach a final equilibrium. But, speaking
by and large, this seems less plausible than the view which associ-
ates it with development; and I believe that this is probably the
attitude of most of those who in recent years have paid attention
to this subject. I should hesitate to say when first it was explicitly
stated. In my own thought its origins are associated principally
with the works of Cassel and Spiethoff and, more recently, of Sir
John Hicks.[1] But I am very prepared to believe that, in the enormous miscellaneous literature of the subject, there may be discovered anticipators. What is important from the point of view
of this survey, however, is not the exact origin of this notion but
the fact that once it is accepted, the theory of growth and the
theory of the cycle acquire a very intimate connection and come
to be treated by similar analytical methods.

10. RE-EMERGENCE OF A THEORY OF AGGREGATES

There is a further development of the last thirty-five years which
must be noticed in this connection.

The Great Depression of the thirties involved downward

[1] See Gustav Cassel, *Theory of Social Economy* (1923) vol. ii, pp.
503 *seq.*, Spiethoff's article on Krisen in the *Handwörterbuch der
Staatswissenschaften*, a translation of which appears in *International
Economic Papers*, no. 3, and Hicks, *A Contribution to the Theory of the
Trade Cycle* (1950).

fluctuations of employment and output so much transcending anything experienced in the course of the trade cycle of the nineteenth century as almost to present a difference of kind rather than degree. It was therefore natural in such circumstances that attention should be directed to the problem of the fundamental determinants of employment and output — a problem which, rightly or wrongly, had been somewhat elided by the assumption of a long-run tendency to reasonably full employment of those resources whose prices were not rigid. It was to the solution of this problem that Keynes directed the powerful constructions of his *General Theory*; and, whatever the imperfections or excesses of particular propositions in that extraordinary work, I think it would now be generally admitted that, since its publication, our outlook on these matters can never be quite the same again. In so far as growth depends on the maintenance of high levels of employment, the theory of economic development has been considerably reinforced.

But the Keynesian analysis was essentially short period and statical. It assumed the existence of given labour and given equipment and, in true-blue Marshallian manner, it gave a comparison of different statical equilibria rather than providing a theory of the path actually taken by change. Hence it was inevitable, especially in the context of the post-war situation with new nations pathetically clamouring to learn the secret of rapid growth, that attempts should be made to transcend this analysis and to provide a full theory of the actual process of development. Hence the constructions of Harrod, Domar, Kaldor and many others, ably analysed by Hahn and Matthews in a famous supplement to the *Economic Journal*, with the debate still continuing.

II. TRANSITIONAL

The narrative of my two last sections has taken us to a point at which what I called the *how* questions have taken precedence over the *why* questions — at which simplified models of interactions take the place of analysis of the fundamental ingredients. As I said at the beginning, it is no part of my intention to trace this last phase in any detail. Even with the aid of Hicks and Hahn and Matthews, it is still too early to be sure of the proper perspective. All that I have tried to do in this last connection has been to show how the one kind of inquiry is related to the other and why at this stage of history we have arrived where we are.

My remaining lectures therefore will be devoted to more detailed analysis of the history of some of the answers to the *why* questions: I shall first proceed to theories of population and returns.

POPULATION AND RETURNS

1. INTRODUCTORY

THE object of this lecture is to trace the history of thought relating to the connection between population growth and economic development. This is not a matter which appears very frequently in the modern discussions of the theory of development although I should hope that we are by now all aware of the truly frightening prospects looming ahead which are due to this factor. But it figures large in earlier thought on our subject. In the classical outlook, to discuss development without considering the tendencies of population growth would have been to omit the most essential ingredient ; and in this respect I am inclined to think that, with all its obvious imperfection, classical thought was of considerably more practical significance than most of the theoretical models of our own day. I make no apology therefore for putting this subject first in my series of more detailed surveys.

2. ALTERNATIVE CHRISTIAN ATTITUDES

It is clear that discussion of population can be traced back very far in history. The learned Stangeland in his *Pre-Malthusian Doctrines of Population* [1], requires no less than 350 pages to assemble utterances on this subject, from ancient Hebrew literature to the Physiocrats and Arthur Young. The idea that there was no such discussion before the publication of the *Essay on the Principle of Population* is entirely unhistorical.

[1] *Op. cit.* New York, 1904.

Much of this discussion, however, has little bearing on development. When St Paul said that 'It is good for a man not to touch a woman' but that it was 'better to marry than to burn', he was making a statement which has had a profound influence on the Christian attitude to relations between the sexes and which affords a mordant glimpse of his own state of mind.[1] But he was not thinking of the relation between numbers and productivity. By way of contrast Luther held that, unless he was naturally or artificially impotent, no man was able to live virtuously without a wife and that only a lack of faith in the Deity could cause any hesitation in entering into matrimony — a point of view which, although implying a belief in an infinite tendency to at least constant returns, obviously sprang from preoccupations which can hardly be labelled as economic.

There remains, however, even at a comparatively early stage, a substantial body of discussion not dominated by theology or dogmatic morality; and it is here that we may begin our survey. As might be expected, the protagonists in these discussions fall into two groups: those who hold that an increase in population is conducive to prosperity and those who are impressed by the danger of pressure on existing resources. It will be convenient to arrange our discussion with this division in mind.

3. EARLY ADVOCATES OF INCREASE

I begin therefore with the thought of those favouring population increase.

But before proceeding further, it is necessary to underline an important distinction — the distinction, namely, between the position of those who regard the increase of population as a *sign* of

---

[1] 1 Cor. 7: 1 and 9. It is perhaps worth noting that later in the chapter he went on to remark that he who gave his virgin daughter in marriage did well but that he who gave her not did better (v. 38). Nothing in the context suggests that this was intended to be humorous.

prosperity and the position of those who regard it as a *cause* thereof. It is quite fundamental not to confuse the two. The position that increasing numbers are a sign of prosperity is perfectly compatible with the view that such an increase is detrimental to income per head. No less an authority than Adam Smith held that 'the most decisive mark of the prosperity of any country is the increase of the number of its inhabitants',[1] a view which derived from his belief that population increase would be greatest when capital accumulation had resulted in wages which for the time being were above subsistence level. But he also believed that if such an increase continued, then sooner or later it tended to reduce wages to the subsistence level which was their eventual destination once capital had ceased increasing faster than labour. The same position is adopted by Malthus himself: 'Increasing population is the most certain possible sign of the happiness and prosperity of a state: but the actual population may be only a sign of the happiness that is past.'[2] But the position that increasing population is a cause rather than a result of prosperity must clearly rest on an entirely different process of reasoning.

What that process was is not always altogether easy to determine. The position we have to examine is chiefly prevalent in the literature of the so-called mercantilist period — using that term in its wider sense; and the arguments for an increasing population involve all sorts of criteria not necessarily relevant to economic development — a strong army, cheap labour, better tax yield and so on. Even where the focus is upon wealth as such, more often than not it is *aggregate* rather than *average* wealth which seems to be the criterion. Thus Child in his *New Discourse of Trade* (1694) advances the proposition that 'Most nations . . . are more or less rich or poor proportionately to the paucity or plenty of their people and not to the sterility or fruitfulness of their lands'.[3] This involves an assumption of an absence of diminishing returns. But

---

[1] Smith, *The Wealth of Nations*, vol. i, p. 72.

[2] Quoted in the *Edinburgh Review* (Jan. 1837) from a fragment of the unpublished tract on *The Crisis*, a censure of Pitt's government written in 1796.   [3] *Op. cit.*, p. 179.

it does not involve development in Adam Smith's sense of an increase in income per head.

Here and there, however, there are to be found arguments which go further. There is a very odd argument by Sir William Temple: 'The true and natural ground of trade and riches is the number of people in proportion to the compass of the ground they inhabit. This makes all things necessary to life dear, and that forces men to industry and parsimony. These customs ... become with time to be habitual. And wherever they are so that place must grow great in traffic and riches.'[1] This certainly assigns a positive role to population increase. But, although not implausible in certain conjectural settings, it lacks much in general applicability.

As might be expected, there is more depth in Petty's *obiter dicta* on the subject. In the *Treatise on Taxes* — surely one of the most wonderful productions of seventeenth-century economic thought — he argues that: 'Fewness of people is real poverty; and a nation wherein are Eight Millions of people, are more than twice as rich as the same scope of Land wherein are Four.'[2] Here is a genuine assertion of an increasing average return to increasing numbers, though it is true that the reason given, 'that the same Governours which are the great charge, may serve near as well, for the greater, as for the lesser number' does not carry great conviction. But elsewhere, in the *Political Arithmetic*, there is reference to the benefits of the division of labour. I therefore see no reason to deny Petty credit for insight into what can truly be said in favour of expansion.

4. ANTICIPATION OF MALTHUS

I turn now to the position of those who argue the dangers of increasing numbers; and here I do not think it necessary to spend

[1] Sir William Temple, 'An Essay upon the Advancement of Trade in Ireland' in *Works* (1814) vol. iii, pp. 2–3.

[2] Sir William Petty, *A Treatise on Taxes*, reprinted in *The Economic Writings of Sir William Petty*, ed. Hull (1899) vol. i, p. 34.

much time on the pre-Malthusian literature. It is true that going back to quite an early stage there are to be found warnings of the pressure of numbers on subsistence and even overt invocations of the ideal of geometrical potentialities of increase. There are hints or more extensive disquisitions on these lines in Machiavelli, Botero and Hobbes. But the impact on thought came from Malthus; and in this context very much enumeration of anticipators would be somewhat otiose.

There are, however, a few names which call for mention.

First I would cite Cantillon whose terse statement that 'Men multiply like Mice in a barn' if they have sufficient subsistence, puts in a nutshell the main burden of the whole Malthusian theory. It is true that he went on to rule himself out of the more normative side of development theory by calmly observing that it was a question outside his 'subject whether it is better to have a great multitude of Inhabitants, poor and badly provided, than a smaller number, much more at their ease; a million who consume the produce of 6 acres or 4 millions who live on the produce of an Acre and a half'.[1] But the pith of the matter is there for anyone who wishes to perceive it.

Next comes poor Sir James Steuart, who had so many interesting ideas but who knew so ill how to express them. In his *Principles of Political Economy* he, too, sees numbers limited by the availability of subsistence, and argues that : 'The generative faculty resembles a spring with a loaded weight which always exerts itself in proportion to the diminution of resistance : when food has remained sometime without augmentation or diminution, generation will carry numbers as high as possible ; if their food is diminished, the spring is overpowered ; the force of it becomes less than nothing, inhabitants will diminish at least in proportion to the overcharge. If on the other hand food be increased, the spring will exert itself in proportion as the resistance diminishes ; people will begin to be better fed ; they will multiply and in proportion as they increase in numbers, the food will become scarce

[1] Richard Cantillon, *Essai sur la Nature du Commerce*, ed. Higgs (1931 edition) pp. 83 and 85. All future references are to this edition.

again.'¹ Here is an argument very much akin to the Malthusian idea of a repressed geometrical rate of potential increase.

Much the most important of the predecessors, however, is Adam Smith, not only because of the clarity of his thought in this connection, but also because it was part of a system which, as we have already seen, was in large measure concerned with development and that according to a criterion — the magnitude of income per head — which is entirely congenial to modern notions. Furthermore, it is arguable that in certain respects the Smithian analysis is more plausible and indeed more realistic than that of Malthus and of greater significance therefore for the theory of development. But of that more later.

The Malthusian element in Smith's analysis is well expressed in the following paragraph from the chapter on Wages in book 1 of *The Wealth of Nations*. 'Every species of animal naturally multiplies in proportion to the means of their subsistence and no species can ever multiply beyond it. But in civilized society it is only among the inferior ranks of the people that the scantness of subsistence can set limits to the further multiplication of the human species; and it can do so in no other way than by destroying a great part of the children which their fruitful marriages produce.'² This follows an account of the effects of poverty on the rearing of children in the course of which it is mentioned that 'it is not uncommon in the Highlands of Scotland for a mother who has borne twenty children not to have two alive'.

But the theory is much more elaborate than this. In stationary conditions, according to Smith, wages are likely to be at what it was customary to call subsistence level, which was in effect enough to maintain the labourer and his wife and enable them to bring up a family such as, taking account of mortality rates, would keep the population constant. But, when accumulation is taking place, wages are likely to be above that level. If the funds 'destined for payment of wages' increase, then 'the scarcity of hands occasions

¹ Sir James Denham Steuart, *An Inquiry into the Principles of Political Economy* (1767) p. 20.
² Smith, *The Wealth of Nations*, vol. i, p. 81.

a competition among masters who bid against one another, in order to get workmen',[1] and this tends to raise wages above subsistence level. And this state of affairs can persist so long as these funds go on increasing. If the increase stops, however, then it is to be expected that the supply of labour will catch up and wages will cease to be high: 'It is not the actual greatness of national wealth, but its continual increase, which occasions a rise in the wages of labour. . . .'[2]

'Though the wealth of a country should be very great, yet if it has long been stationary, we must not expect to find the wages of labour very high in it. . . . If in such a country the wages of labour had ever been more than sufficient to maintain the labourer, and to enable him to bring up a family, the competition of the labourers and the interest of the masters would soon reduce them to the lowest rate which is consistent with common humanity. . . .'[3]

'The liberal reward of labour, therefore, as it is the effect of increasing wealth, so it is the cause of increasing population. To complain of it, is to lament over the necessary effect and cause of the greatest public prosperity.'[4]

It is this possibility, namely that for long periods as a result of influences operating on the demand side, wages may be above subsistence level, that distinguishes Smith's view from that originally held by Malthus; and it was this possibility which, as we shall see, offered to a later generation of classical economists the possible prospect of permanent emancipation from poverty.

5. THE ESSAY ON POPULATION: THE FIRST VERSION

It is now time to turn to Malthus whose work in this field, whether it is regarded as acceptable or not, dominates the thought of this time and indeed all subsequent thought on the subject. But to get it in proper perspective it is necessary to distinguish sharply

[1] Smith, *The Wealth of Nations*, vol. i, p. 70.
[2] Ibid., p. 710.   [3] Ibid., p. 73.   [4] Ibid., p. 83.

between the position adopted in the first (1798) edition of his famous book and that position as modified thereafter.

The first edition of the *Essay on the Principle of Population* was essentially, as its sub-title implies,[1] a polemic against the Utopian hopes current among the enthusiasts of the French Revolution. Malthus says, 'I have read some of the speculations on the perfectibility of man and of society with great pleasure. I have been warmed and delighted with the enchanting picture which they hold forth. I ardently wish for such improvements. But I see great, and, to my understanding, unconquerable difficulties in the way to them. These difficulties it is my present purpose to state. . . .'[2]

He begins with what he calls 'two postulata'. 'First, that food is necessary to the existence of man. Secondly, that the passion between the sexes is necessary and will remain nearly in its present state.'

After some slight elucidation of the second, necessitated by Godwin's odd belief that the passion in question might in time be extinguished, he goes on to advance his main proposition: 'that the power of population is infinitely greater than the power in the earth to provide subsistence for man'[3] and to draw the conclusion that 'By that law of our nature which makes food necessary to the life of man, the effects of these two unequal powers must be kept equal' which 'implies a strong and constantly operating check on population from the difficulty of subsistence'.[4]

He then discloses the nature of this check: 'Through the animal and vegetable kingdoms, nature has scattered the seeds of life abroad with the most profuse and liberal hand. She has been comparatively sparing in the room, and the nourishment necessary to rear them. The germs of existence contained in this spot of earth, with ample food and ample room to expand in, would fill

[1] The full title was *An Essay on the Principle of Population as it affects the Future Improvement of Society; with Remarks on the Speculations of Mr. Godwin, M. Condorcet, and other writers.*

[2] *Op. cit.* (1798) p. 7.

[3] Ibid., p. 13. [4] Ibid., p. 14.

millions of worlds in the course of a few thousand years. Necessity, that imperious all-pervading law of nature, restrains them within the prescribed bounds. The race of plants and the race of animals shrink under this great restrictive law. And the race of man cannot, by any efforts of reason, escape from it. Among plants and animals its effects are waste of seed, sickness, and premature death. Among mankind, misery and vice.'[1]

Later on he distinguishes two manifestations of this check: 'a foresight of the difficulties attending the rearing of a family acts as a preventative check, and the actual distresses of some of the lower classes, by which they are disabled from giving the proper food and attention to their children, acts as a positive check to the natural increase of population.'[2] Both, however, operate in ways involving either misery or vice.

It is easy to see that on this view the prospects of improvement — development in the sense of increases in income per head, unaccompanied by misery and vice — are negligible, save for a very short period. Malthus provides a demonstration of this in an examination of Godwin's position regarding property and other supposedly inimical institutions such as marriage. Let us suppose, he argues, that all such obstacles are swept away. 'War and contention cease. Unwholesome trades and manufacturers do not exist. . . . Simple healthy and rational amusements take place of drinking, gaming and debauchery. . . . All men are equal. . . . The spirit of benevolence will divide and produce according to their wants.'[3] 'I cannot conceive', he says, 'a form of society so favourable on the whole to population',[4] and he then proceeds to investigate the probable effects of successive periods of doubling. At the end of the second period 'a quantity of food equal to the frugal support of twenty-five millions would have to be divided among twenty-eight millions'.[5] The pressure recreates the evils of the past. 'The mighty law of self-preservation expels all the softer and more exalted emotions of the soul.' 'In so short a period as within fifty years, violence, oppression, falsehood,

[1] Ibid., pp. 14–15.   [2] Ibid., pp. 62–3.   [3] Ibid., pp. 181–2.
[4] Ibid., p. 184.   [5] Ibid., p. 189.

misery, every hateful vice, and every form of distress, which
degrade and sadden the present state of society seem to have been
generated by the most imperious circumstances, by laws inherent
in the nature of man and absolutely independent of all human
regulations.'[1]

6. THE ESSAY ON POPULATION: SECOND THOUGHTS

But Malthus did not stop at this point. In the second (1803)
edition of his *Essay* — which in so many respects was virtually a
new book — he admits the possibility of a check which does not
involve misery and vice, the famous moral restraint. Edwin
Cannan used to suggest that he may have discovered from his own
experience that a deferment of marriage until late in his thirties
did not involve either misery or vice. At any rate he now admitted
that such a check was conceivable.

The consequences for the theory of development were momen-
tous. If it were true that the pressure of population on subsistence
could be eased by action which was not morally reprehensible,
then it was no longer true that, theoretically at least, the human
race was condemned — to use the words of the first edition, 'to a
perpetual oscillation between happiness and misery, and after
every effort [to] remain still at an immeasurable distance from the
wishes for goal'.[2] This did not mean any great concession to
Godwinian and philosophical anarchy; for under that system,
Malthus still thought, the sense of personal responsibility which
alone could lead to moral restraint would be absent. But it did
mean that, given suitable institutions and social habits, the possibility of improvement could not be absolutely denied.

It is important to realise, however, that by moral restraint
Malthus did not mean deliberate control of conception. Condorcet
had hinted at such a possibility in his *Esquisse*; and Malthus went

[1] Ibid., pp. 190–1.   [2] Ibid., pp. 2–3.

out of his way vehemently to deny any suspicion of his counte-
nancing such expedients.[1]   It is quite clear that, on his classification,
contraceptive practices would figure, not as moral restraint, but
as vice.   It was not surprising therefore that the hopes which he
based on 'moral restraint' were distinctly moderate, even though
in this second edition he had attempted, to use his own words,
'to soften some of the harshest conclusions of the first essay'.[2]
His vision of the future was not very rosy.   In his correspondence
with Senior,[3] he did indeed concede that 'as education and knowledge are extended, the probability is that these evils [the pressure
of population against food] will practically be mitigated, and the
conditions of the labouring classes be improved'.   But such an
admission did not colour his main treatment of the subject.   And
indeed so long as the only permissible check to population pressure
was of the kind he envisaged, this attitude was surely abundantly
justified.

But his scruples did not communicate themselves to everybody.
Bentham had already suggested in cold print the use of contraceptive devices as a cure for poverty[4] and, among his followers James
Mill and Francis Place, the whole Malthusian analysis, far from
suggesting perpetual condemnation of the majority of the human
race to misery at subsistence level, became a healing diagnosis
pointing the way to emancipation and progress.   If, as Adam Smith
had explained, accumulation could be maintained so as to keep
wages above subsistence level long enough for the working classes
to acquire a taste for 'comforts and enjoyments', and if there
existed means whereby, without improbable austerities, they could
limit numbers, then progressive improvement could be hoped for.
James Mill contented himself with the broad generalisations of
his article on colonies in the Supplement to the *Encyclopaedia*

---

[1] In the appendix printed in Malthus, *Additions to the Fourth and
Former Editions* (1817) pp. 292–3.

[2] *Op. cit.* (1803) p. viii.

[3] Appendix to N. W. Senior, *Two Lectures on Population* (1831) pp.
82–83.

[4] Bentham, *Works*, ed. Bowring (1843) vol. viii, pp. 367–8.

Britannica: 'If the superstitions of the nursery were discarded, and the principles of utility kept steadily in view, a solution might not be very difficult to be found.'[1] But Francis Place went more directly to the point. In his *Illustrations of the Principle of Population* he deliberately recommended contraception as the solution to the Malthusian problem; and he risked — and suffered — much public opprobrium by a printed leaflet giving practical details: 'If', he argued, 'it were once clearly understood, that it was not disreputable for married persons to avail themselves of such precautionary means as would, without being injurious to health or destructive of female delicacy, prevent conception, a sufficient check might at once be given to the increase of population beyond the means of subsistence; vice and misery, to a prodigious extent, might be removed from society, and the object of Mr. Malthus, Mr. Godwin, and of every philanthropic person, be promoted by the increase of comfort and intelligence and of moral comfort, in the mass of the population. . . . It is time . . . that those who really understand the cause of a redundant, unhappy, miserable, and considerably vicious population, and the means of preventing the redundancy, should clearly, freely, openly and fearlessly point out the means.'[2]

This attitude spread among the bolder spirits of the age. It is said, though complete confirmation is lacking, that the young John Stuart Mill spent a night in a police station, having been caught distributing information of this nature. The movement for deliberate control of population pressure, in our own day the best hope of saving humanity from the worst effects of the population explosion, thus takes its rise in the heart of the classical system.

[1] James Mill, *The Article Colony*, reprinted separately (1828) pp. 12–13.

[2] Francis Place, *Illustrations of the Principle of Population* (1822) pp. 165, 173–4. See also J. A. Field, 'The Malthusian Controversy' and 'The Early Propagandist Movement in English Population Theory' in *Essays on Population* (Chicago, 1931).

7. DIMINISHING RETURNS AND POPULATION

To return to more analytical matters. As we have seen, the
Malthusian pessimism was based upon the alleged inability of food
production to keep pace with the potentialities of the increase of
numbers. Malthus tried to drive this home by his celebrated
comparison between ratios: 'Population, when unchecked, increases in geometrical ratio. Subsistence increases only in an
arithmetical ratio',[1] and he illustrated this by the juxtaposition of
the series:

$$1, 2, 4, 8, 16, 32, 64 \ldots$$
and $$\qquad 1, 2, 3, 4, 5, 6, 7, 8 \ldots$$

for numbers and food respectively.

This is a very loose way of putting things, and from a technical
point of view it is not difficult to shoot holes in it. It is easy enough
to think of geometrical ratios which, within any period sensible
to consider, advance very slowly, and arithmetical ratios which
advance very briskly. Moreover, the way Malthus argues, the
possibilities of technical improvement are subsumed in the arithmetical ratio along with the ultimate scarcity of the land factor,
which is analytically very confusing indeed.

Nevertheless I see no reason whatever to question Marshall's
view that the habit of speaking in terms of an arithmetical ratio
was 'really only a short way of stating the utmost that he thought
any reasonable person could ask him to concede', and that 'what
he meant, stated in modern language, was that the tendency to
diminishing return, which is assumed throughout his argument,
would begin to operate sharply after the produce of the island had
been doubled. Doubled labour might give doubled produce:
but quadrupled labour would hardly treble it: octupled labour
would not quadruple it.'[2] I know that this interpretation has been

---

[1] *Op. cit.* 1st ed. (1798) p. 14.
[2] Alfred Marshall, *Principles of Economics*, 8th ed. (1920) p. 179 fn.
All further references are to this edition.

questioned, particularly by Cannan.[1] But since, even in the first edition, there are hints of the idea of diminishing returns,[2] since Malthus himself was one of the first explicitly to formulate it in connection with the Corn Law controversy,[3] and since he invokes it quite overtly in his *Summary View of the Principles of Population*,[4] this degree of scepticism seems to be unwarranted.

But be this as it may, the controversy regarding protection to agriculture, which took place in this country as the Napoleonic Wars came to an end, threw up formulations of the so-called Law of Diminishing returns in agriculture which were entirely apt for this purpose. This had, indeed, been clearly stated at a much earlier date by Turgot, but in a setting, however, which more or less guaranteed the absence of any influence on thought.[5] But from this period onward it becomes a central feature of classical analysis to assume that, in the absence of technical change, to use West's words, 'each equal additional quantity of work bestowed on agriculture yields an actually diminished return, and, of course, if each additional quantity of work yields an actually diminished return, the whole of the work bestowed on agriculture in the progress of improvement yields an actually diminished proportionate return'.[6] It is true that in this context the so-called law was used chiefly to establish propositions in the theory of value and distribution. But its applicability to the discussion of production was obvious and it was not long before it was so employed.

[1] 'To imagine that the *Essay on the Principle of Population* was ever based on the law of diminishing returns is to confuse Malthusianism as expounded by J. S. Mill with Malthusianism as expounded by Malthus.' Edwin Cannan, *Theories of Production and Distribution*, 3rd ed. (1922) p. 144.

[2] *Op. cit.* pp. 106–7 fn.

[3] See especially Malthus, *On the Nature and Process of Rent* (1815) pp. 38–9.

[4] Reprinted in D. V. Glass, *Introduction to Malthus* (1953) p. 122.

[5] It was in remarks on a prize essay by Saint-Péravy submitted to the Royal Agricultural Society at Limoges, *Œuvres*, ed. Daire (1844) vol. i, pp. 420–1.

[6] Sir Edward West, *Essay on the Application of Capital to Land* (1815) pp. 6–7.

Thus we find it as the fourth of Senior's famous Elementary Propositions of the Science and as the development thereof, namely, that 'Additional Labour when employed in Manufactures is *more*, when employed in agriculture is *less* efficient in production', a proposition on which there will be more to say later on. But it reaches its fullest usage in John Stuart Mill's *Principles* where it is one of the main pillars of the system.[1] Mill recognises the possibility of technical changes which alters the whole position of the returns function. He concedes that something of this sort must have been happening over long stretches of history. He pays lip-service to the existence of an 'antagonizing principle' in the division of labour. But throughout one feels that, for him, the probability of diminishing returns to further increases of population is a dominating consideration and that one of the main hopes of improvement lies in the restraint of this increase.

8.   INCREASING RETURNS AND THE SIZE OF THE MARKET

It is now time to return to the other side of the picture. The earlier writers who had advocated increasing numbers as a mean to increased prosperity certainly erred when they spoke as if there were no limits to this effect — as if returns increased, or remained constant, indefinitely. But there was certainly something in what they had to say, something more than what appeared in the Malthusian analysis. All history, all common sense, suggests that it is not reasonable to argue as if returns necessarily begin diminishing at a very early stage in the increase of numbers or that all increases in actual returns per head are due to technical improvements. Any comprehensive theory of the subject must take account of that and provide some explanation thereof.

As might be expected, the germs of such an explanation are to be found in *The Wealth of Nations*. The explanation of the advantages of the division of labour which we find in the very first chapter is of course not original; some discussion of this subject goes back

[1] *Op. cit.* pp. 173–85.

to Plato and Aristotle. Nor is it analytically complete: it omits both the advantages deriving from the appropriate use of fundamental differences in innate ability and those deriving from what Torrens called territorial division of labour. But it sets forth with such vividness the significance for the progress of opulence, to use Smith's phrase, of increasing division of labour that it must always be regarded as the *locus classicus* of the subject and as the exposition which made the division of labour the central feature of the social system from the economic point of view. Who can forget the peroration in which the position of the poor man in a society practising division of labour is contrasted with that of the wealthiest member of a primitive community. 'Compared, indeed, with the more extravagant luxury of the great, his accommodation must no doubt appear extremely simple and easy; and yet it may be true, perhaps, that the accommodation of a European prince does not always so much exceed that of an industrious and frugal peasant, as the accommodation of the latter exceeds that of many an African king, the absolute master of the lives and liberties of ten thousand naked savages.'[1]

Adam Smith does not at this stage explicitly link increasing division of labour with increasing population. But he does link it with the extent of the market. 'As it is the power of exchanging', he says, 'that gives occasion to the division of labour, so the extent of this division must always be limited by the extent of that power, or, in other words, by the extent of the market.'[2] The chapter (chapter iii) in which this occurs is comparatively short; but from an analytical point of view it is certainly one of the most significant in the book. For, as the late Allyn Young observed in a paper which is one of the most important contributions of the last fifty years, his 1928 address to the British Association, *Increasing Returns and Economic Progress*, it is the key to the problem of increasing returns and economic progress.[3]

Now the extent of the market does not depend wholly on the extent of the population; it depends also on the magnitude of

[1] *Op. cit.* vol. i, p. 14.
[2] Ibid., p. 19.   [3] Reprinted in the *Economic Journal* (Dec. 1928).

income per head and upon the degree to which individual demands are similar.　Moreover, as Adam Smith was at pains to argue at length in book II, the growth of division of labour depends in part upon accumulation, which is certainly not determined only by the mere fact of population growth.　Nevertheless, there is clearly some connection; one has only to reflect upon the development of transport systems to realise the dependence of their profitability on a certain degree of density of population in the areas connected; and clearly the economies of mass-production are only to be achieved in a *milieu* where there is mass consumption to absorb the product.　It is therefore not unexpected that at the end of his chapter on the wages of labour, Smith should at last explicitly associate the benefits of division of labour with the existence of what he calls a 'great society'.　'The owner of the stock which employs a great number of labourers', he says, 'necessarily endeavours, for his own advantage, to make such a proper division and distribution of employment, that they may be enabled to produce the greatest quantity of work possible.　For the same reason he endeavours to supply them with the best machinery which either he or they can think of.　What takes place among the labourers in a particular workshop, takes place for the same reason, among those of a great society.　The greater their number, the more they naturally divide themselves into different classes and sub-divisions of employment.　More heads are occupied in inventing the most proper machinery for executing the work of each, and it is, therefore, more likely to be invented.'[1]

9.　THE CONCEPTION OF AN OPTIMUM POPULATION

It cannot be said that this part of Smith's analysis was at all well integrated into the work of the majority of the classical economists.

[1] *Op. cit.* vol. i, p. 88.　See also the section on the 'Effects of the Progress of Improvement upon the real Price of Manufactures', vol. i, pp. 242–6, and the remarks on the 'Causes of the Prosperity of new Colonies', vol. ii, p. 66 f.

Needless to say, they all expatiated on the advantages of the division of labour, usually with explanations more comprehensive and analytically persuasive than Smith's. But it was not linked up with the theory of exchange as in *The Wealth of Nations* — still less was there any conspicuous emphasis on the connection between the degree of the division and the extent of the market and the numbers of the people. The proposition of Senior's which I have already quoted, relating to diminishing returns in agriculture and increasing returns in manufacture, is developed independently of the discussion of division of labour; and in any case, it depends on a false dichotomy — there can be division of labour in agricultural operations as in manufacture; and it is not the nature of the operations but rather the fixity of the supply of natural resources which gives rise to diminishing returns in the sense relevant to this part of the theory. John Stuart Mill does indeed mention the connection between division of labour and the extent of the market[1] and elsewhere he speaks of a principle antagonistic to the law of diminishing return: the progress of improvements in production, which certainly includes the idea of increasing resort to mass production.[2] But as we have seen, this does not greatly influence his views on population. In one place he actually allows himself to say that 'A greater number of people cannot, in any given state of civilization, be collectively so well provided for as a smaller'.[3] And this is all the more odd in that elsewhere he lends the weight of his great authority to the colonisation schemes of Wakefield, whose main justification was the necessity of achieving a certain degree of density of population if the advantages of division of labour were to be realised.[4]

In course of time, however, a more balanced view developed.

[1] Mill, *Principles of Political Economy*, pp. 129–30.

[2] Ibid., pp. 177–85, especially p. 182.

[3] Ibid., p. 188.

[4] See E. G. Wakefield's *Letters from Sydney* (1829) and the *Art of Colonization* (1849) *passim*. I have given some account of Wakefield's views and their influence in Robbins, *Robert Torrens and the Evolution of Classical Economics* (1958) pp. 153–181.

It is perhaps doubtful whether the analytical depth of Smith's treatment was paralleled until the publication of the article by Allyn Young to which I have already drawn attention; it has always been an amazing thing to me that this path-breaking development should have attracted so comparatively little notice. But in Sidgwick's *Principles* — a greatly underrated book which has suffered unduly by comparison with Marshall's great work — the problem is discussed in a way which puts both aspects of population growth in an unexceptional perspective, with the increasing advantages of division of labour contrasted with the limitations on agricultural and extractive industry imposed by scarcity of natural resources.[1] And at a later date a sharper edge was put on the same analysis, by both Cannan and Wicksell[2] working, so far as I know, quite independently, with the conception of a size of population which, in any given state of technique, is optimal; on either side of it returns per head would be less. As Cannan puts it: 'If we suppose all difficulties about the measurement of returns to all industries taken together to be somehow overcome, we can see that, at any given time, knowledge and circumstances remaining the same, just as there is a point of maximum return in each industry, so there must be in all industries taken together. If the population is not large enough to bring all industry up to this point, returns will be less than they might be: if on the other hand population is so great that the point has been passed, returns are again less than they might be.'[3] This does not bring out enough the contrast between the increasing returns due to division of labour and diversification of industry and the diminishing returns due to the

---

[1] Henry Sidgwick, *Principles of Political Economy*, 3rd ed. (1901) pp. 150–1.

[2] Cannan's first formulation is to be found in his *Elementary Political Economy* (1888) pp. 21–5. It was subsequently elaborated in successive editions of his *Wealth: A Brief Explanation of the Causes of Economic Welfare*. K. Wicksell's thoughts on the subjects are to be found in the German edition of his lectures, *Vorlesungen über Nationalökonomie* (1913), book I, p. 50.

[3] Cannan, *Wealth*, 3rd ed. (1928) p. 58.

fixity of natural resources. But it does provide an appropriate formal framework.

10. LIMITATIONS OF THIS CONCEPTION

So far so good. But while it is intellectually satisfying to have disentangled the conflicting views of the past in this way, it is very necessary to realise how far short of easy practical applicability this concept of an optimal population still is. Four points in particular may be noted.

In the first place, it assumes a constant range of technical knowledge and a constant capital. Now, while a constant range of technical knowledge is a fairly familiar abstraction, constant capital, in the sense appropriate to this analysis, most decidedly is not. For it involves the further assumption that, as population varies, the actual physical shape of the constant capital varies too so that, at each point, it assumes the most suitable manifestation. This is perhaps not impossible to grasp intellectually. But actual variations of this sort would take so long to work themselves out that the assumption that they can happen puts an immense strain on the governing assumption that other things remain equal.

Secondly, it is a conception which is only applicable without much further complication to the circumstances of a closed community. Whether an open community is over- or under-populated depends not only on the size of its material resources and the extent of the division of labour which would be practised if it were a closed community; it depends also on the extent to which it is able to practise division of labour with the rest of the world. And this in turn depends upon what is happening elsewhere and the extent of intercommunication. If we look, for instance, upon London as an open community, it might be hard to argue that income per head there would be higher, other things being equal, if its population were less. But if we imagine London hedged in by all sorts of restrictions on trade, this might easily be the case.

Whether or not this island is over-populated in this sense now, it is clear that it might easily become so if in one way or another the terms of trade were to turn seriously against us.

Thirdly, it involves all the usual index number problems and further problems of its own besides. For if one is to measure changes in income per head with changing population in any intelligible way, it is necessary to assume that as population changes the constituent elements remain more or less equal-natured in their relative demand and supply functions. Now there seems little harm in doing this for small changes. But when we consider changes of the size appropriate to considerations of the relation of population to resources, this imposes a much greater strain on our credulity.

Finally, we must realise that the criterion of income per head is a criterion which takes account only of what may be called discriminate benefit: the constituents of real income which may be matched with the expenditure of individuals. All so-called neighbourhood effects, either positive or negative, are left out by this method of counting. Yet it is arguable that where variations of population are concerned, this is a very grave omission. John Stuart Mill hated the thought that the countryside would become insufficiently lonely.[1] The inhabitants of so-called new countries are said to

---

[1] 'A population may be too crowded, though all be amply supplied with food and raiment. It is not good for man to be kept perforce at all times in the presence of his species. A world from which solitude is extirpated is a very poor ideal. Solitude, in the sense of being often alone, is essential to any depth of meditation or of character; and solitude in the presence of natural beauty and grandeur, is the cradle of thoughts and aspirations which are not only good for the individual, but which society could ill do without. Nor is there much satisfaction in contemplating the world with nothing left to the spontaneous activity of nature; with every rood of land brought into cultivation, which is capable of growing food for human beings; every flowery waste or natural pasture ploughed up, all quadrupeds or birds which are not domesticated for man's use exterminated as his rivals for food, every hedgerow or superfluous tree rooted out, and scarcely a place left where a wild shrub or flower could grow without being eradicated as a weed in the name of improved agriculture. If the earth must lose that great

long for the atmosphere of a metropolis.

Nevertheless, when all these qualifications have been taken into account, I submit that it may still be contended that quite important clarifications of thought have taken place. We can state why in some circumstances more population is conducive to development and why in others it is a menace. We may not be sure of our judgment in regard to, say, present-day western Europe. But we can be reasonably sure of the condition of the United States, say, in 1776, or of India at the present day.

portion of its pleasantness which it owes to things that the unlimited increase of wealth and population would extirpate from it, for the mere purpose of enabling it to support a larger, but not a better or a happier population, I sincerely hope, for the sake of posterity, that they will be content to be stationary, long before necessity compels them to it.'
Mill, *Principles of Political Economy*, p. 756.

ACCUMULATION
AND EFFECTIVE DEMAND

I. INTRODUCTORY

In this lecture I propose to deal with capital accumulation and its role in the history of the theory of economic development. At first sight this might seem to be a banal theme to occupy the greater part of a lecture. In the present phase of affairs we are so used to regarding accumulation as a good thing and ample capital provision as an almost indispensable prerequisite of development, that it might be thought that, so far as history is concerned, the only thing to do is to discover the man who first said so and then to take note of non-stop applause from that date to the present day.

But of course it is not so. Outside the completely authoritarian society where the creation of capital goods results simply from decrees regarding the allocation of labour and the use of existing resources, the accumulation process is a complex business involving decisions to save on the one side and decisions to create capital stocks and equipment on the other; and these decisions are not necessarily harmonious and do not necessarily involve equal benefits for development. The history of the theory of accumulation is in fact a mixed history of approbation and disapprobation, the rights and wrongs of which have only been sorted out in our own day. And this is not just a matter of discovering the possibility of financial disharmonies involving what Robertson called savings running to waste: as we shall discover, there have been influential figures denying the desirability of real accumulation beyond a certain point, either because of its limited productivity or because

44

of alleged disharmonies between the investment process and effective demand.[1] There is no need therefore to fear shortage of material in the time available for discussion.

2. PRE-SMITHIAN THEORIES

I do not think that in this connection we need spend much time on eighteenth-century thought prior to Adam Smith. The theory of circulation of the Physiocrats provides some background to underconsumption theories at a later stage.[2] And, as Dr Vickers has shown, there is much in the works of writers such as Barbon and Berkeley which can be interpreted as anticipating some modern propaganda in favour of spending.[3] But on the specific question of the advisability — or inadvisability — of saving and its effects on development there is not a great deal which is sufficiently precise to deserve notice in a bird's-eye survey, such as this lecture.

It is perhaps desirable, however, to say a word about the position of Bernard de Mandeville in the famous *Fable of the Bees*. This, you may remember, was roped in by Keynes to figure large in his scratch list of anticipations of the central propositions of the *General Theory*: and it is not difficult to see why, to the *épatiste* mood in which that list was drawn up, the doggerel contrasts should have had especial piquancy. In the vicious hive where all sorts of evils worked together for good:

> 'The root of evil, avarice,
> That damn'd ill natured, baneful vice,
> Was slave to prodigality,
> That noble sin: whilst luxury

[1] The use of the term 'investment' in this context is quite deliberate. See below in the discussion of Malthus for its justification.

[2] On this aspect of Physiocratic Thought, Professor Meek's interesting essay in his *Economics of Physiocracy* (1962) should be consulted.

[3] See his *Studies in the Theory of Money 1690–1776* (1960).

>Employed a million of the poor,
>And odious pride a million more.'

Whereas, when the hive had turned virtuous:

>'But Oh ye Gods? What Consternation
>How vast and sudden was th'Alteration.
>In half an Hour, the Nation round,
>Meat fell a Penny in the Pound . . .
>For 'twas not only that They went,
>By whom vast sums were yearly spent
>But Multitudes that lived on them
>Were daily forced to do the same
>In vain to other Trades they'd fly;
>All were o'erstocked accordingly.'[1]

— which is all very good fun, and perhaps not without some short-term applicability to a period of deep depression. As Hayek and others have shown, there is much in Mandeville which is profound and illuminating. But this skit on saving is not much more than a vivid presentation of the eternal tradesman's cry that spending is good for trade. It is not surprising, therefore, that Adam Smith, who in other connections took so much from Mandeville in his analysis of the general interconnection of self-interest and mutual benefit, should have taken nothing in this respect and indeed should have become the chief exponent of the contrary view.

3. ACCUMULATION IN THE SMITHIAN SYSTEM

What that view was is best discovered if we fasten our attention on the title of chapter iii, book ii, of *The Wealth of Nations*. This book is devoted to the 'Nature, Accumulation and Employment

[1] Bernard de Mandeville, *The Fable of the Bees*, ed. Kaye (1924) pp. 25, 28, 32.

of Stock', and chapter iii, which contains the central analysis, is headed 'Of the Accumulation of Capital or of Productive and Unproductive Labour'; and in this context it is the latter phrase which is significant. It is neglect of this conjunction which has led to all sorts of unnecessary confusion.

To grasp why this is so, it is important to understand what Smith meant by productive as opposed to unproductive labour. He did not mean, as did the Physiocrats, labour engaged in agricultural or extractive occupations; he was at great pains to repudiate this. But he did mean labour which produces something 'which lasts for some time at least after that labour is past' — labour which fixes and realizes itself in some particular subject or vendible commodity' in contrast to that which consists in the performance of services which 'perish in the very instant of their performance, and seldom leave any trace or value behind them, for which an equal quantity of service could afterwards be procured'.[1]

Now we all know the difficulties to which this particular use of the word 'productive' can give rise. Are they not the stock-in-trade of hundreds of first-year primers and lecture courses? We all know that if the adjective 'productive' is understood to mean productive of *income* wealth, then this restriction to production of material objects is seriously misleading — the standard examples of the 'false' contrast between the labour of the man who digs coals out of the earth and the man who puts them on the fire, or the labourer making shoes and the man polishing them, have been repeated *ad nauseam*; as has the more fundamental point that labour does not *produce* matter but only *rearranges* it. But this is not what Smith was driving at. By productive he meant productive of *capital* wealth; and when he laid it down that the proportion between productive and unproductive labour was one of the two circumstances determining the wealth of nations — the other being the extent of the division of labour — he was simply using another way of saying that development depends on the maintenance and accumulation of capital. The chapter heading

[1] *Op. cit.*, vol. i, pp. 313–14.

makes this quite clear — or perhaps I should say it should have done so, since there has been more misinterpretation of Smith's intentions in this connection than of most other parts of the classical system.

Accumulation, thus conceived, is depicted as desirable because the capital stock to which it gives rise renders labour more productive — 'facilitates and abridges' is Smith's phrase — and because it sustains the development of the division of labour. There can clearly be no objection to the first of these propositions: that which relates to the increased productivity brought about by the use of machines and other forms of fixed capital. And although there has been much cavilling at the way in which Smith put the second — the alleged support of the division of labour — I confess I cannot see any ground for denying the broad good sense which underlies it. Is it really to be supposed that division of labour in an advanced society would have reached anything like its present state without a massive accumulation of capital?[1]

The question therefore arises, what makes new accumulation possible? What causes an increase in the proportion of productive to unproductive labour?

On this Smith's answer is unequivocal; and it is of great importance for the main perspective of this survey: 'Capitals', he says, 'are increased by parsimony and diminished by prodigality and misconduct. Whatever a person saves from his revenue he adds to his capital, and either employs it himself in maintaining an additional number of productive hands, or enables some other person to do so, by lending it to him for an interest. As the capital of an individual can be increased only by what he saves from his annual revenue or his annual gains, so the capital of a society, which is the same with that of the individuals who compose

---

[1] A great deal of heavy criticism has been brought to bear on Smith's unwise statement that before a man takes to weaving, a stock of food etc. must be available to keep him until the product is completed (see, e.g., Cannan, *Theories of Production and Distribution*, 3rd ed. (1922) p. 81 *seq.*). But this does not touch the point that if weaving takes time, it has to be sustained in cash or kind by *advances* against the final product.

it, can be increased only in like manner.'[1]

All this is quite straightforward, as are the more detailed observations on the frugality and prodigality of persons and of states which follow at a later stage. But what follows immediately is the famous proposition that 'What is annually saved is as regularly spent, and nearly in the same time too; but it is consumed by a different set of people'; and to judge by its history, this cannot be regarded as by any means immune from misunderstanding.

We may notice first that it has been the subject of severe criticism on the ground that the capital to which saving gives rise is not consumed — or not consumed nearly in the same time as the saving itself. Thus Cannan argues that, on this way of putting things, 'it is not the new canal or new waterworks which are said to be saved but the food, clothing and lodging consumed by the productive labourers who produce them'. This is true enough. But surely it is pretty superficial. In a preceding chapter Adam Smith had very clearly indicated durable instruments of this kind as part of the capital stock of society; it is not really plausible to argue as if he had forgotten between chapters this very obvious circumstance. In this connection it is very important to distinguish between the *process* of accumulation — the setting productive labour to work — and the *end-product* thereof, the increased stock. When Adam Smith spoke of what is saved, he was referring to the process; when he spoke of the increase of capitals he meant the latter. This may be a trifle inconvenient; on the whole it is a pity that he put things this way. But it does not necessarily imply confusion of thought.

There is, however, a further implication here which is of much greater significance for the understanding of Smith's thought and the subsequent development of theory. When it is said that what is saved is consumed, it is thereby implied that there is no hoarding, no gap between planned saving and investment. The money which, but for parsimony, would have been spent as wages for unproductive labourers, in Smith's sense of that term, is spent instead on the services of productive labourers. This may not

[1] *Op. cit.*, vol. i, p. 320.

be an exactly accurate way of representing the accumulation process — there may be other items of expenditure not covered by this formula. But the significance as regards any possible leakages is unequivocal; and this is fundamentally inportant. As we shall see in all discussion of the effects of saving, for a very long time to come it was taken for granted — both by those who believed in the inevitable beneficence of saving and by those who did not. Even when analysis took much more account of the separation between the decision to save and the decision to invest — as in that article by William Ellis in the *Westminster Review*[1] to which John Stuart Mill attached such importance — the suggestion of a gap which could have adverse effects on income and expenditure was absent.

4. JOHN RAE AND CAPITAL THEORY

There is no need to discuss in detail the further treatment by classical orthodoxy of this body of theory. Smith's main propositions were taken over more or less as they were propounded in *The Wealth of Nations*. The benefits of accumulation were set forth in the third of Senior's Four Elementary Propositions of the Science, namely, 'That the powers of labour and other instruments which produce wealth may be indefinitely increased by using their products as the means of further production': and the origin of accumulation in the use of resources for remote as distinct from immediate results, which Smith had described as parsimony, he designated as abstinence — a splendid opening for jocularity on the part of Marx and Lasalle.

There is, however, one development outside the literature of the main tradition which is so remarkable that it deserves some special notice: I refer to the treatment of what he calls 'The Nature of Stock' in John Rae's most unjustly neglected *New*

[1] William Ellis, *The Effects of the Employment of Machinery*, Westminster Review V, Jan. 1826, 201–30. Mill's allusion is in his *Principles*, p. 736.

Principles of Political Economy. The main purpose of this book was a critique of the alleged identification of individual and social interest in *The Wealth of Nations* and a plea for the fostering of infant industries in certain stages of development. But in the course of this argument there occur a series of chapters on the theories of capital and invention which are quite unique in the literature of the time, both for their originality and their insight.

Rae commences his treatment of 'the Nature of Stock' with a disquisition strongly anticipating Irving Fisher,[1] on the 'course of events and the connexion of one with another' as the focus of economic calculation. Capacity to anticipate the probability of future developments and to make provision for modifying them is the 'chief distinction between man and the inferior animals'. All means for influencing the course of events by changing 'the form or arrangement of material objects' are termed instruments. The stock of instruments therefore includes all wealth existing at any moment of time.[2]

So much is mere terminology — although terminology involving some fairly deep insights. But after a certain amount of discussion of a purely descriptive character of the formation and exhaustion of instruments, Rae now ascends to an entirely new plane in an analysis of instruments according to their rate of return over cost. His position is perhaps best described in terms of the relevant chapter heading: '*Every Instrument may be arranged in some part of a series of which the orders are determined by the proportion existing between the Labour expended in the formation of instruments, the capacity given to them and the time elapsing from the period of formation to that of exhaustion.*'[3] This is developed, with copious illustrations of instruments producing events equivalent to double their costs in short periods or medium periods or longer; and there is much ingenious analysis showing how returns not fitting

[1] Cf. the opening sentence of Irving Fisher, *The Theory of Interest* (New York, 1930), 'Income is a series of events', and the overt reference to Rae.

[2] John Rae, *New Principles of Political Economy* (Boston, 1834) pp. 80–94.   [3] Ibid., p. 100.

into so simple a series may be recalculated so as to make them do so. And in the next chapter there is formulated a sort of law of diminishing returns to investment in terms of a delay of the doubling point as accumulation proceeds. 'The capacity which any people can communicate to the materials they possess, by forming them into instruments, cannot be indefinitely increased, while their knowledge remains stationary, without moving the instruments forward continually onwards in the series A B C etc.'[1] He illustrates this with reference to the varying degrees of durability which can be imparted to houses. 'A dwelling might be lightly run up of wood, lath, mud, and plaster like the unsubstantial villages that Catherine of Russia saw in her progress through some part of her dominions. Another of the same size, accommodation, and appearance, that might last two or three centuries, might be constructed by employing stone, iron and the most durable woods, and joining them and compacting them together with great nicety and accuracy.'[2] He thinks that 'there is no assignable limit to the extent of the capacity which a people, having attained considerable knowledge of the qualities and powers of the materials they possess, can communicate to them without carrying them out of the series A B C etc., even if that knowledge remains stationary'.[3]

Having elaborated his investment function, Rae then turns to the grand question, to what extent will it be exploited? The answer to this he finds in time preference or, to use his own, rather than the modern, terminology, the effective desire of accumulation: 'The formation of every instrument', he says, 'implies the sacrifice of some smaller present good, for the production of some greater future good. If, then, the production of that future greater good, be conceived to deserve the sacrifice of this present smaller good, the instrument will be formed, if not, it will not be formed. According to the series in which we have arranged instruments, they double the cost of their formation in one, two, three, etc. years. Consequently, the order to which in any society the formation of instruments will advance, will be determined by

---

[1] Ibid., p. 109.   [2] Ibid., p. 110.   [3] Ibid., p. 109.

the length of the period, to which the inclination of its members to yield up a present good, for the purpose of producing the double of it at the expiration of that period, will extend, according as it stretches to one, two, three, twenty, forty, etc. years will the formation of instruments be carried, to the orders, A, B, C, T, *n*, etc. and, at the point where the willingness to make the sacrifice ceases, there the formation of instruments must stop.'[1] The substantial identity of this solution with Fisher's equality of the marginal rate of time preference and the marginal rate of return over cost leaps to the eye. The conception of the margin is lacking; but the broad architecture is the same.

Having provided a formal solution of this problem, Rae proceeds to provide psychological amplification. Were life eternal and 'the dictates of reason' the sole guide to action, there would be no limit to accumulation 'till our utmost wishes were supplied'.[2] But this is not so. There is a conflict between the passion for immediate self-indulgence and reflection both on our own future needs and the needs of the family: and the result will vary according to the relative strength of these influences. Moreover, where society itself is unstable and the uncertainties of the future are great, the desire to accumulate is weakened. These generalities are then tested by historical examples. The imprudence of communities of hunters is contrasted with the greater prudence of cultivators, the habits of the Red Indians with those of the white settlers in North America, the lack of durability of instruments and the height of interest rates in the China of Rae's day, with the solidity of capital construction and the lowness of rates in parts of Europe.

Even here, after many pages of vivid illustration, Rae has not finished his analysis. A further section discusses the relation between the rate of return on investment and what we should call liquidity preference: 'Every man', he says, 'must be more unwilling to run the risk of having a sum of money lying useless by him, by how much greater the amount of the returns he could have by turning it to the formation of instruments. If then, in the society of which any man is a member, instruments are not far

[1] Ibid., p. 119. [2] Ibid., p. 119.

C

removed from the first orders of our series, when they soonest double the expenditure of their formation, he will rather risk the inconvenience of having too little money by him, than the loss of having a sum in his coffers long unemployed, which might have been converted into instruments yielding large returns. But if, in the society of which he is a member, instruments are far removed from the first orders of our series, he will be disposed to reserve a greater amount in the hopes of making more by some advantageous bargain, than he could by expending it on the formation of any instrument.'[1] And this in turn leads to an analysis of the functions of money and credit, discussion of which, however, would carry us beyond the subjects of this lecture.

Rae's book fell more or less dead from the press. Senior knew of it and recommended it to Mill who read it and incorporated substantial parts of it into the relevant section of his *Principles of Political Economy*, comparing the importance of Rae's treatment of accumulation with that of Malthus on population. But there the matter ended, save for an Italian translation, probably completely unknown to the author, which appeared in Ferrara's *Biblioteca dell'economista*, vol. xi. For any further notice this extraordinary contribution had to wait for its rediscovery until the time of the discussions of Bohm Bawerk's *Positive Theory of Capital*: and even today, although Irving Fisher dedicated his great *Rate of Interest* 'To the Memory of John Rae who laid the Foundations upon which I have endeavoured to build', it has never received the attention it deserves — which must be my excuse for dwelling upon it at such length in this lecture.[2]

[1] Ibid., p. 178.

[2] There can be little doubt that in recent years some of this neglect has been due to the grotesque misadventure that when it was rediscovered the discoverer, C. W. Mixter, caused it to republished under the absurd title — for a publication of 1834 — *The Sociological Theory of Capital*, rearranged on a principle of his own devising which effectively concealed Rae's main intention. So that for another half-century the original, one of the rarest works of antiquarian economic items, remained more or less unobtainable. Fortunately the publication by the Toronto University Press of R. W. James' *John Rae, Political Economist*

5. THE LAW OF MARKETS

We must now turn to another development which strongly influenced the main classical approach to the problem of saving. Adam Smith's propositions that 'what is annually saved is . . . as regularly consumed', with its implied denial of the likelihood of hoarding, received a powerful reinforcement from the development of the argument that, in the last analysis, supply was the source of demand and that aggregate production was, so to speak, its own market.

The originator of this proposition was the French economist, J. B. Say, from whom it received the somewhat pretentious title of the 'Law of Markets' (Loi des Débouchés) and after whom, in modern discussions, it has often been called Say's Law. The original statement in the *Traité d'Économie Politique* is a good deal less rigorous than some of its applications by subsequent writers. Say recognised the possibility of hoarding — there is a footnote reference thereto on the third page of the chapter in which the so-called Law is set forth. But, although he does not specifically say so, his argument assumes that for practical purposes this can be ignored. He begins by recalling the view frequently expressed by business men that their difficulty lies not in the production but in the disposal of their wares. He comments on this that there cannot be a demand for the products of any one tradesman unless others have obtained the requisite money by the sale of theirs. But money is only desired as a means of purchasing. The ultimate reason why sales of any one commodity are slack, therefore, is that there is a lack of production elsewhere. The mere circumstance of the creation of one product immediately opens a vent for other products. It is true that, owing to failure to anticipate demand correctly, there may be a glut of particular commodities. But this must be paralleled by equivalent scarcity elsewhere. 'The

(Toronto, 1965), which contains a facsimile reproduction of the original and an almost simultaneous reprint by Augustus Kelly has corrected this disability.

general demand for produce is brisk in proportion to the activity of production.'[1]

This way of putting things achieved a wide reception in this country, originally through its use for polemical purposes by James Mill. In the course of public discussion of the probable effects of the Napoleonic Blockade, William Spence, a writer of Physiocratic views, had published a pamphlet entitled *Britain Independent of Commerce*, the purport of which was to show that since agriculture was the sole source of wealth, the destruction of our foreign trade was a matter of little importance. Mill replied to this in a work entitled *Commerce Defended* and among his arguments there emerged an exposition of the views regarding aggregate demand to which he had already drawn attention in a review of Say's book.[2]

For reasons which do not follow clearly from the main intention of his book, Spence had argued that the expenditure of the landlord class was an essential condition of prosperity. Were they to save, then the lessening of aggregate demand would narrow the field of profitable employment and depression would follow. It should be noted that he goes out of his way to dismiss hoarding as an explanation of this effect.

In the first part of his critique, Mill deals with this position on Smithian lines. 'Let not Mr. Spence be alarmed. Let him rest in perfect assurance that the whole annual produce of the country will be always very completely consumed, whether his land holders choose to spend or accumulate.'[3]

But later on, warming to the controversy, he puts things Say's way: 'No proposition ... in political economy seems to be more certain than this which I am going to announce, how paradoxical soever it may at first appear ... and if it be true, none undoubtedly can be deemed of more importance. The production of commodi-

[1] J. B. Say, *A Treatise on Political Economy*, trs. Prinsep (1821) vol. i, p. 180.

[2] In the *Literary Journal* (Apr. 1805) pp. 412–25.

[3] James Mill, *Commerce Defended*, in *Selected Economic Writings*, ed. Winch (1966) p. 129.

ties creates, and is the one and universal cause which creates, a market for the commodities produced. . . . When goods are carried to market what is wanted is somebody to buy. But to buy, one must have wherewithal to pay. It is obviously therefore the collective means of payment which exist in the whole nation that constitute the entire market of the nation. But wherein consist the collective means of payment of the whole nation? Do they not consist in its annual produce, in the annual revenue of the general mass of its inhabitants? But if a nation's power of purchasing is exactly measured by its annual produce, as it undoubtedly is . . . the more you extend the annual produce, the more by that very act, you extend the national market, the power of purchasing and the actual purchases of the nation. . . . The demand of a nation is always equal to the produce of a nation.'[1]

Much the same argument reappears in Mill's *Elements*.[2] It was warmly approved by Ricardo; and despite what to us must seem its glaring *lacunae*, it was taken very seriously by the majority of classical economists and had wide influence on thought and, if not on policy, at least on recommendations of policy.

6. MALTHUS AND UNDER-CONSUMPTION

It was not universally accepted, however. The influence of Spence was not great. But there were others of higher standing who repudiated the Smithian eulogy of parsimony and urged the great danger of over-saving.

Among these we must first mention the Earl of Lauderdale, whose *Inquiry into the Nature and Origin of Public Wealth* is one of the most notable of the neglected works of early nineteenth-century political economy. Chapter iv of this work is a frontal

[1] Ibid., p. 135–6.
[2] James Mill, *Elements of Political Economy*, in *Selected Economic Writings*, ed. Winch (1966). See especially ch. iv, section iii: 'That Consumption is co-extensive with Production', pp. 326–37.

attack on Smith's dictum that frugality increases, and prodigality diminishes public wealth — the title alone conveys the scepticism of its approach: 'Of the Possibility of Increasing Wealth by any other means than those by which it is produced'. Lauderdale admits the existence of a use for capital equipment. But he is of the opinion that in any given state of knowledge there are fairly near limits to this use and hence to the utility of accumulation: 'Man's invention in the means of supplementing labour', he says, 'may give scope in the progress of society for the employment of an increased quantity [of capital]; but there must be at all times a point determined by the existing state of knowledge in the art of supplanting and performing labour with capital, beyond which capital cannot profitably be increased and beyond which it will not naturally increase; because the quantity when it exceeds that point, must increase in proportion to the demand for it, and its value must of consequence diminish in such a manner as effectually to check its augmentation. . . .'[1] He thinks the mischief done by parsimony is fortunately almost uniformly counteracted by prodigality. But he argues that in so far as the praise of parsimony has given rise to sinking funds and the like, its effects must be wholly bad.

Much more significant than anything that Lauderdale had to say was the attitude of Malthus, whose position, as the author of the *Essay on the Principle of Population* and the close friend of Ricardo, guaranteed a hearing for his every utterance on matters of political economy. Malthus was not so severe in condemnation as Lauderdale: 'Lord Lauderdale appears to have gone as much too far in depreciating accumulation as some other writers in recommending it', he said.[2] But he did argue very strongly that beyond a certain point saving defeated itself by a reduction of effective demand and indeed that a substantial proportion of what he called unproductive consumption was needed if the economy were not to fall into depression.

It is well known that Keynes thought that in Malthus he had

[1] *Op. cit.* (Edinburgh, 1804) pp. 227–8.
[2] Malthus, *Principles of Political Economy* (1820) p. 352 n.

discovered an anticipator of his own analysis. 'If only Malthus, instead of Ricardo, had been the parent stem from which nineteenth-century economics proceeded, what a much wiser and richer place the world would be today', [1] he wrote; and certainly, if we have regard to the superficial look of many of Malthus' statements, this impression seems to be justified. Thus he writes, 'We see in almost every part of the world vast powers of production which are not put into action', and he goes on to explain this phenomenon by saying that 'from the want of a proper distribution of the actual produce, adequate motives are not furnished to continued production.... I don't at all wish to deny that some person or persons are entitled to consume all that is produced' he continues, 'but the grand question is whether it is distributed in such a manner between the different parties concerned as to occasion the most effective demand for future produce: and I distinctly maintain that an attempt to accumulate very rapidly which necessarily implies a considerable diminution of unproductive consumption, by greatly impairing the usual motives to production must prematurely check the progress of wealth.'[2]

How reasonable that sounds, given the background of the contemporary depression — and how modern! Yet closer examination shows that, so far from deriving from one analysis in the mode of Keynes, in fact it derives from an analysis which is absolutely antithetical. For the essence of the Keynesian analysis is that the attempt to save which is not matched by a corresponding attempt to invest, leads to downward pressure on incomes and output, but that if the corresponding investment actually takes place, then all is well. Whereas for Malthus the position is exactly reversed: it is the fact that savings are spent and that investment actually takes place which is responsible for trouble. The Malthusian theory of under-consumption, like the theories of J. A. Hobson three-quarters of a century later, proceeded on the assumption that savings were in fact invested; and it based its

[1] J. M. Keynes, *Essays in Biography*, 2nd ed. (1951) p. 120.
[2] This occurs in a letter to Ricardo. See Ricardo, *Works*, vol. ix, p. 10.

analysis of depression on that fact. In the Keynesian terminology, it traced depression, not to attempted savings which failed to get invested, but to investment which actually took place. Any doubt on this must surely be dispelled by Malthus' vehement protestation: 'No political economist of the present day can by saving mean mere hoarding; and beyond this contracted and inefficient proceeding, no use of the term, in reference to national wealth, can well be imagined, but that which must arise from a different application of what is saved, founded upon a real distinction between the different kinds of labour which may be maintained by it.'[1]

Hence, although many of Malthus' *obiter dicta* both on the causes of depression and the implausibility of Say's Law seem to derive from intuitions in many ways sounder and more in touch with contemporary reality than those of his opponents, it is difficult to contend that they rested on a very convincing analytical position. It is no accident therefore that on the intellectual plane it was Ricardo rather than Malthus who was triumphant. For although Ricardo's assumption of no hoarding, no saving running to waste, was unjustified: yet once it was accepted, as it was accepted by Malthus, the logic of the argument was his. Like most of the other underconsumptionists of the period — with the exception of Lalor[2] — Malthus failed to vindicate his position because his theory was defective.

7. JOHN STUART MILL on THE INFLUENCE OF CONSUMPTION ON PRODUCTION

There was thus an intellectual *impasse* in the discussion of this

[1] Malthus, *Principles of Political Economy* (1820) p. 32.

[2] See B. A. Corry's account of this very interesting writer in his *Money Saving and Investment in English Economics 1800–1850* (1962) pp. 106–7, 145–51. This work is a mine of information, splendidly mustered, on many of the topics discussed in this lecture.

subject. Those who perceived that the economic system was subject to ups and downs not explained by existing theory were precluded from explaining this phenomenon by the acceptance of an assumption — the absence of fluctuations in the demand for money — which in fact ruled it out. While those who reasoned logically from this assumption were left with a conclusion — the conclusion that there could be no such thing as a general glut — which was manifestly out of touch with reality.

Now a hint of the way in which these contradictions might be resolved is to be found in a comparatively early work by Torrens. In his *Essay on the Production of Wealth* (1821), in the course of an explanation of the way in which the over-production of a particular commodity may have adverse effects throughout the economy, he alludes to the possibility of changes in the relative valuation of money and goods. 'On every occasion of glut or general stagnation', he says, 'the desire of turning goods into money is rendered more intense than the desire of turning money into goods, and the proportion in which prices will fall in relation between the quantity of commodities and the amount of currency will be altered.' And he goes on to explain why in such circumstances 'the rate of interest may rise while the profits of stock fall to nothing.'[1] But the main credit for breaking this *impasse* must go to an inner member of the so-called orthodox school; no less a person than John Stuart Mill, who stands to the end of the classical period as Adam Smith stood to the beginning. In his paper *On the Influence of Consumption on Production*, published in his *Essays on some Unsettled Questions of Political Economy*, he provided an analysis which, while conceding nothing to the general argument against saving and accumulation, broke through the sterile logic of Say's Law and showed how, from time to time, a holding back of expenditure might produce the appearance of a general glut. It is worth spending a little time following his argument in detail.

The essay begins with a strong denial of the general position of the under-consumptionists. Adam Smith's fundamental

[1] R. Torrens, *op. cit.* pp. 421–2. See Robbins, *Robert Torrens and the Evolution of Classical Economy* (1958) p. 176 *seq.*

C 2

proposition is reaffirmed: 'The person who saves his income is no less a consumer than he who spends it. He consumes it a different way; it supplies food and clothing to be consumed, tools and materials to be used, by productive labourers.'[1] This principle and the corollary that what is needed for economic progress is production, not consumption, he thinks is now well established. But there remains the task 'of seeing that no scattered particles of important truth are buried and lost in the ruins of exploded error.' He therefore addresses himself to inquire into 'the nature of the appearances which have given rise to the belief that a great demand, a brisk circulation, a rapid consumption are a cause of national prosperity'.[2]

The basis of this belief, he suggests, is to be found in the more rapid turnover of capital which is consequent on a period of 'brisk demand'. But such periods 'are also the periods of greatest production: the national capital is never called into full employment but at these periods'. 'This, however,' he goes on to argue, 'is no reason for desiring such times; it is not desirable that the whole capital of the country should be in full employment. For, the calculations of producers and traders being of necessity imperfect, there are always some commodities which are more or less in excess, as there are always some which are in deficiency. If therefore the whole truth were known, there would always be some classes of producers contracting, not extending their operations. If *all* are endeavouring to extend them, it is a certain proof that some general delusion is afloat. The commonest cause of such delusion is some general or very extensive rise of prices (whether caused by speculators or the currency) which persuades all dealers that they are growing rich. . . .'[3]

Mill then says that business is in fact liable to alterations of excessive hopes or fears so that 'general eagerness to buy and

[1] *Op cit.*, p. 263. The *Essays on some Unsettled Questions of Political Economy* (1844) are reprinted in the Toronto edition of Mill's works in the volumes entitled *Essays on Economics and Society* 1967, and all further references are to this source.   [2] Ibid., p. 264.
[3] Ibid., p. 274.

general reluctance to buy succeed one another in a manner more or less marked, at brief intervals. Except during short periods of transition . . . either the principal producers of almost all the leading articles of industry have as many orders as they can possibly execute or the dealers in almost all commodities have their warehouses full of unsold goods.' He continues: 'In the last case, it is commonly said that there is a general superabundance.' How is this to be reconciled with the statement that such a state of affairs is inconceivable? This leads Mill to a searching examination of the arguments developed by J. B. Say and his father.

The proposition that supply is at the same time demand, he says, 'is evidently founded on the supposition of a state of barter. . . . When two persons perform an act of barter, each of them is at once a seller and a buyer. He cannot sell without buying. . . . If however we suppose that money is used, these propositions cease to be exactly true . . . the effect of the employment of money . . . is that it enables this one act of interchange to be divided into two separate operations. . . . Although he who sells, really sells only to buy, he need not buy at the same moment when he sells; and he does not therefore necessarily add to the *immediate* demand for one commodity when he adds to the supply of another. . . . There may be . . . a very general inclination to sell with as little delay as possible, accompanied with an equally general inclination to defer all purchases as long as possible. This is always actually the case in those periods which are described as periods of general excess.'[1]

Thus, 'to render the argument for the impossibility of an excess of all commodities applicable to the case in which a circulating medium is employed, money must itself be considered as a commodity. It must undoubtedly be admitted that there cannot be an excess of all other commodities, and an excess of money at the same time.' This saves the case for J. B. Say and his father from the formal point of view. But equally it points clearly to its inapplicability in ordinary conversation.

Mill concludes by emphasising that 'the argument against the possibility of general over-production is still quite conclusive so

[1] Ibid., pp. 275–6.

far as it applies to the doctrine that a country may accumulate capital too fast.' He submits, however, that this is not incompatible with the view that 'as there may be a temporary excess of any one article considered separately, so there may be of commodities generally, not in consequence of over-production but of a want of commercial confidence'.[1]

I think it must be agreed that this is a very remarkable article. It does not, it is true, deal with the possibility that, because of some hold-up in the capital market, attempted savings may run to waste for considerable periods. But at least it provides, what earlier statements of the orthodox classical position had conspicuously failed to provide, a possible explanation of the appearance of general over-production, without surrendering the general position that the effects of accumulation are beneficial. It would not have satisfied Malthus. But at least it put a plausible gloss on Smith and Ricardo.

8.   THE NEO-CLASSICAL TRADITION

It cannot be said that Mill's article had any conspicuous impact. I do not know any reference to it in the relevant contemporary literature. Mill himself, in writing his *Principles*, was obviously careful to avoid the dogmatism which his article had been intended to dissolve; and, reading between the lines, one can detect the fundamental outlook which it expressed.[2] But he made no special point of it, as might have been expected; and what is said has certainly little of the cutting edge of the original article.

Nevertheless something of this attitude seems to have entered the main tradition. You do not find in the literature of the next seventy-five years much of the dogmatism which sprang from the Law of Markets, although there was a professor here in this

---

[1] Ibid. pp. 278–9.
[2] *Op. cit.* See especially p. 540 *seq.*

university of Oxford, the fabulous Bonamy Price,[1] who seems to have devoted some effort to proving the impossibility of under-consumption. And I imagine that if, for instance, Marshall had been challenged on the subject, he would have replied more or less on the lines of Mill's article. Certainly that is the impression that I get from the account of the ups and downs of trade in the early jointly written *Economics of Industry*,[2] often referred to by Dennis

[1] Apparently he was a very corpulent man, and according to an account which I had from the lips of Edgeworth, after the apolaustic meals of the Oxford Political Economy Club, he would sit back, arms resting forwards on an almost globular abdomen, stating in a high-pitched voice the sacred dogma: 'There can be no general glut.'

[2] 'But though men have the power to purchase they may not choose to use it. For when confidence has been shaken by failures, capital cannot be got to start new companies or extend old ones. Projects for new railways meet with no favour, ships lie idle, and there are no orders for new ships. There is scarcely any demand for the work of navvies, and not much for the work of the building and the engine-making trades. In short there is but little occupation in any of the trades which make Fixed capital. Those whose skill and capital is Specialised in these trades are earning little, and therefore buying little of the produce of other trades. Other trades, finding a poor market for their goods, produce less; they earn less, and therefore they buy less; the diminution of the demand for their wares makes them demand less of other trades. Thus commercial disorganization spreads, the disorganization of one trade throws others out of gear, and they react on it and increase its disorganization.

'The chief cause of the evil is a want of confidence. The greater part of it could be removed almost in an instant if confidence could return, touch all industries with her magic wand, and make them continue their production and their demand for the wares of others. If all trades which make goods for direct consumption agreed to work on and to buy each other's goods as in ordinary times, they would supply one another with the means of earning a moderate rate of profits and of wages. The trades which make Fixed capital might have to wait a little longer, but they too would get employment when confidence had revived so far that those who had capital to invest had made up their minds how to invest it. Confidence by growing would cause itself to grow; credit would give increased means of purchase, and thus prices would recover. Those in trade already would make good profits, new

Robertson. The same can be said of Pigou's early work on fluctuation in the first edition of the *Economics of Welfare* and of Lavington's monograph *The Trade Cycle*. The fact is that the nature of the great controversies of the half-century after Mill's death was not such as to focus attention on the accumulation process as such. There was much discussion of the value of money and possible ways of maintaining greater stability — bimetallism, the tabular standard for contracts, the compensated dollar. There was much discussion of the nature of capital and the necessity of interest. But apart from what Keynes called the underworld of heresy, which, for the most part, simply reiterated the sort of thing which Spence and Malthus had said before,[1] there was little discussion of the macro-economic effects of saving or the benefits to development of accumulation.

9. STAGNATION THEORY

It was therefore not until the inter-war period with its hyper-inflation and the great depression, that attention was directed in a large way to aggregate problems of this sort. From this, as you know, after much controversy resulting largely from the contributions of Keynes and Robertson, in the English-speaking world, and from Wicksell's pupils at Stockholm, there emerged substantial clarification. We know now how to define the relationships of planned saving and planned investment, in such a way that we can say formally that until planned saving is equal to planned investment, it has all the virtues — and more — that classical

companies would be started, old businesses would be extended; and soon there would be a good demand even for the work of those who make Fixed capital.' Alfred and Mary Paley Marshall, *The Economics of Industry* 1879 pp. 154–5.

[1] An exception should be made for N. Johannsen whose *A Neglected Point in Connection with Crises* (New York, 1908) seems to have got very near what is now held to be the truth of the matter.

orthodoxy attributed to it and that, after that point when it is in excess, we walk so to speak through the looking-glass and, in the first approximation at least, it produces the evil effects which the under-consumption theorists thought they saw but so signally failed to explain. We know too about the possibilities — I will not say probabilities — of blockages in the adjustment mechanism of the capital market at very low rates of interest; and we can certainly set forth the comparative statics of the whole subject with a simplicity and precision discontinuously better than anything previously available.

I will not attempt any detail in dealing with this phase of history. It would take a course of lectures in itself to disentangle the contributions of the various participants and the rights and wrongs of the sometimes embittered controversies. As for the main propositions, are they not the stable fare of most introductory courses of lectures nowadays, often to the serious neglect of even more fundamental parts of the subject?

There is, however, one aspect of our subject which is very conveniently dealt with in this connection, the question, namely, of the nature of the investment productivity functions. Does the curve of the marginal efficiency of investment descend gradually or steeply? How near in any given state of knowledge are the limits to the possible benefits of accumulation?

Discussion of this question goes far back. Lauderdale's scepticism concerning the utility to a farmer of 'accumulating a hoard of spades, ploughs and other utensils of husbandry infinitely greater than he could use' can be interpreted as an argument for a steeply declining schedule; and if he and Malthus, relying upon such an assumption, had put their argument for the dangers of under-consumption in terms of stickiness in the capital market in the shape of a sluggish investment demand confronted with falling profit rates and an inelastic saving schedule deriving from ingrained habits of thrift, it would have been at least logically consistent, whether or not it had empirical justification.

Later on in the classical period something like this began to happen. Gibbon Wakefield supported his campaign for systematic colonisation with Cassandra-like warnings of the probable effects of a declining rate of profit at home; and, somewhat surprisingly, his analysis was approved by John Stuart Mill, subject only to the reservation that it was presented as being 'in contradiction to the principles of the best school of preceding political economists, instead of being, as they really are, corollaries from these principles, though corollaries which perhaps would not always have been admitted by those political economists themselves'.[1] One can certainly agree with the afterthought: to judge from some of his remarks to Malthus,[2] Ricardo would have been horrified and so probably would have been Mill's father. It is worth noting, however, that they were wholeheartedly adopted by Robert Torrens, the survivor of the first generation of the nineteenth-century classical school.[3]

It is clear that the analytical concepts of the Keynesian models are, logically speaking, neutral in this connection; they can exhibit a state of affairs in which the incentive to invest falls off rapidly or one in which it declines very slowly. But it is true that Keynes himself was prone to pessimistic views in this connection. He found it difficult to conceive the inventions which could keep the marginal efficiency of investment high for very long; and he did not much believe in the alleged greatly increased openings for investments at lower rates of interest. 'Today and presumably for the future', he wrote, 'the schedule of the marginal efficiency of capital is, for a variety of reasons, much lower than it was in the nineteenth century. The acuteness and the peculiarity of the contemporary problem arises, therefore, out of the possibility that the average rate of interest which will allow a reasonable level of employment is one so unacceptable to wealth owners that it cannot be readily established merely by manipulating the quantity

---

[1] Mill, *Principles of Political Economy*, pp. 735–6.

[2] He clearly thought that profits could decline to the stationary state minimum without any disturbance to anybody. See his letter to Malthus, *Works*, vol. ix, p. 24.

[3] See Robbins, *Robert Torrens and the Evolution of Classical Economics* (1958) pp. 153–81.

of money.'[1] The effect of this on some of his contemporaries was quite remarkable. As a prelude to one of the most astonishing runs of prosperous development in human history, the literature of the subject in the United States resounded with warnings of ultimate stagnation. The days of the frontier were over. The expansion of population was at an end. The war indeed provided an interruption of this process. But the prospect was that, after a brief restocking boom, hopeless depression and deflation would set in, unless alleviated by very wise policies. The evil heritage of an age-long eulogy of prudence and thrift would at last make itself felt.

Well, things haven't turned out that way. And certainly in most countries of the world the conduct of policy in the last quarter of a century would have been immensely easier had the will to save been much greater rather than less. It is possible to argue that some at least of the pressure on resources which has caused the world inflation has been due to rearmament expenditure and that, but for this, some of the gloom of yesterday would have had more justification. But it is difficult to believe that this is the only explanation. At any rate, in a world in which growth has become an almost sacred word and in which league tables are compiled showing what percentage of GNP in each country is devoted to investment, it would be difficult to argue that, for the time being at least, the importance of accumulation for development is in any danger of being neglected.

[1] Keynes, *The General Theory of Employment, Interest, and Money* (1936) p. 308.

EDUCATION AND THE GROWTH OF KNOWLEDGE

1. INTRODUCTORY

IN the two preceding lectures I have been concerned with the history of thought regarding variations in population and accumulation in relation to economic development. I have said nothing concerning variations in the quality of populations or the stock of knowledge at their disposal. Yet clearly these are influences of great significance in the causation of economic development. Material investment without the skill to utilise it is apt to be unprofitable; and the incentive to invest depends much on the march of technical knowledge. It is therefore a matter of considerable interest to determine how such factors have figured in the speculations of the past. Accordingly they will be the subject of the present lecture. I shall deal first with the history of thought regarding the quality of the population, which will involve mainly thought concerning education in this connection. Then I shall proceed to discuss a little the evolution of ideas about the importance of knowledge in the process of economic development and the systematic advancement thereof.

2. THE QUALITY OF THE POPULATION: BIOLOGICAL THEORIES

The quality of the population is obviously a compound of nature and nurture. What men and women are depends partly upon what they bring into the world and partly on what has been added to it by education and experience. On the former of these influences a great deal has been written, scarcely any of it of any value whatever. We know — or we should know — that individuals do differ markedly from one another in original gifts and dispositions. No parent or teacher can plausibly contend that all the differences in achievement of the children under his care are due to education and environment, either in the home or in the school. But, if we are honest, we must admit that we know little more than that. The subject is not insusceptible of investigation, but any worthwhile work still lies mostly in the future.

This has not prevented a great number of people who should have known better from writing a great deal of pseudo-scientific nonsense, or worse, on this particular subject. Aristotle's famous vindication of slavery is the first of a portentous series of assertions about national and racial differences which, without any basis in scientific method, have given respectability to the prejudices of the ignorant and justified many odious practices. We may perhaps accept his view that some are born to lead and others to be led: it is the sort of banality which lends sham profundity to pretentious pronouncements. But when we find that, by some fortunate accident of biology, the Greeks fall into the former class and others into the latter, we are in the realm of a form of dogmatism which is as remote from any attempt at scientific demonstration as it is morally contemptible. The only intellectual interest in this very poor section of the *Politics* is the admission, totally out of key with the bogus biology, that if machines were clever enough, if they were like the tripods of Hephaestus which 'entered self-moved the conclave of the gods', then there would be no need for slaves and slavery.

The classical tradition would have none of this. It is an extraordinary instance of the effect of psychological theories on practical judgment that, rejecting with Locke the belief in innate ideas, and accepting the view that the mind comes into the world as *tabula rasa*, they should have attributed all, or nearly all, differences in human beings to education and environment. Thus Adam

Smith was able to assert that 'the difference between the most dissimilar characters, between a philosopher and a common street porter, for example, seems to arise not so much from nature as from habit, custom and education;'[1] and the Ricardean theory of value, with its persistent neglect of the influence of the scarcity of different kinds of skill, can only be made at all plausible by the assumption that the differences are all assimilable to differences of investment in education. John Stuart Mill actually justified the writing of his *Autobiography* partly on the ground that it would show what attention to education would do for a boy of very ordinary talents.[2]

As an approximation to reality, it is difficult to believe that this assumption of virtual natural equality has much more plausibility than the assumptions of crude racial inequalities. It is surely as improbable that the qualities which went to the writing of Newton's *Principia* or *The Wealth of Nations* were all due to education and environment, as that Greeks were natural leaders and the 'barbarians' natural slaves. The significant difference between the two positions lies, not in the sphere of factual accuracy, for both are fairly obviously false, but rather in the sphere of implications for action. The one leads to the caste society or the gas chamber, the other to an emphasis on the importance of education which,

[1] He goes on to say: 'When they came into the world and for the first six or eight years of their existence they were, perhaps, very much alike and neither their parents nor playfellows could perceive any remarkable difference. About that age, or soon after, they come to be employed in different occupations. The difference of talents comes to be taken notice of, and widens by degrees, till at last the vanity of the philosopher is willing to acknowledge scarce any resemblance.' *The Wealth of Nations*, vol. i, pp. 17–18. An admirable humility in one who himself was a philosopher. But it irresistibly recalls the fact that Smith was a bachelor.

[2] 'If I had been by nature extremely quick of apprehension, or had possessed a very accurate and retentive memory, or were of a remarkably active and energetic character', he wrote, 'the trial would not be conclusive. But in all these natural gifts I am rather below than above par: what I could do, could assuredly be done by any boy or girl of average capacity and healthy physical constitution.' *Autobiography* (1873) p. 30.

in individual instances, may be exaggerated or misleading but which, as regards the great mass of the population, is perhaps not likely to be overdone. Which implication is to be preferred is, as the methodological bores would have us say, a matter of value judgment.

3. EDUCATION AS INVESTMENT

I turn then from these nebulous and misleading generalisations about nature to the more tangible subject of nurture.

The influence of the institution of the family in this respect is clearly of the utmost importance. But it received singularly little attention in the economic thought of the past. Plato, we know, wished to abolish the family, at least for the class of rulers; and Aristotle's exposition of the disadvantages of such an abolition is among the best things in the *Politics* and has not been without continuing influence on thought. But in the traditions of political economy, as it has developed since the Renaissance, the family is conspicuous by its absence. There are honourable exceptions: in Edwin Cannan's admirable *Wealth*, for instance, it receives due attention. But for the most part, in spite of its obvious importance as the unit, not only for the formulation of a substantial proportion of consumers' demand but also for the training of a large part of the population, it is more or less neglected, or at least taken for granted. There is therefore little to report on the history of thought in this subject.

It is otherwise with education outside the family. The measurement of the economic effects of education is indeed a subject on which quantitative precision is lacking, even at the present day. But emphasis on its qualitative importance is conspicuous in the literature of the last two centuries.

It was not always thus, however. The thought of the mercantilist period, although recognising the importance of special skills, tended to blow very cold on the idea of general education for the majority of the population. As Furniss has conclusively shown in his important book on *The Position of the Laborer in a System of Nationalism*, advocacy or defence of low wages, so unjustly attributed to the classical school by twentieth-century sciolists, was the prevalent attitude of a substantial number of the writers of this period; and the idea of education which might make the common labourer discontented with his lot was antipathetic to this attitude.

Thus Mandeville in the *Essay on Charity and Charity Schools*, which is an integral part of the full edition of *The Fable of the Bees*, could not be more explicit: 'In a free Nation where Slaves are not allow'd of, the surest Wealth consists in a Multitude of laborious Poor; for besides that they are the never-failing Nursery of Fleets and Armies, without them there could be no Enjoyment, and no Product of any Country could be valuable. To make the Society happy and People easy under the meanest Circumstances, it is requisite that great Numbers of them should be Ignorant as well as Poor. . . . The Welfare and Felicity therefore of every State and Kingdom require that the Knowledge of the Working Poor should be confined within the Verge of their occupations, and never extended (as to things visible) beyond what relates to their Calling. . . . Reading, Writing and Arithmetic are very necessary to those whose Business require such Qualifications, but where People's livelihood has no dependence on these Arts, they are very pernicious to the Poor, who are forced to get their Daily Bread by their Daily Labour.'[1]

Similar sentiments are expressed even more concisely by an anonymous author quoted by Furniss: 'The charity school is another universal nursery of idleness: nor is it easy to conceive or invent anything more destructive to the interests and the very foundation principles of a nation entirely dependent on its trade and manufactures than the giving of an education to the lowest class of her people that will make them condemn those drudgeries for which they were born.'[2]

[1] Mandeville, *The Fable of the Bees*, ed. Kaye (1924) vol. i, pp. 287–8.
[2] *Op. cit.* (Boston, 1920) p. 148.

With the coming of classical economics a radically different outlook emerges. In the famous chapter on the Division of Stock in book II of *The Wealth of Nations*, Adam Smith puts expenditure on the education and training of human beings on all fours with other kinds of investment and classifies the result thereof, 'the acquired and useful qualities of all the inhabitants or members of society', as one of the forms of fixed capital: 'The acquisition of such talents', he writes, 'by the maintenance of the acquirer during his education, study, or apprenticeship, always costs a real expense, which is a capital fixed and realised, as it were, in his person. Those talents, as they make part of his fortune, so do they likewise of that of the society to which he belongs. The improved dexterity of the workman may be considered in the same light as a machine or instrument of trade which facilitates and abridges labour, and which, though it costs a certain expense, repays that expense with a profit.'[1]

The principle, so stated, of the economic importance of an instructed working population thenceforward became a central position of classical political economy. If we take McCulloch, often represented as insensitive and reactionary, we find him thus underlining its significance in interpreting the contrast between developed and undeveloped economies: 'Much stress is uniformly and justly laid on the efficacy of the machines which man has constructed to assist him in his undertakings: but he is himself the most important of all machines, and every addition made to his skill and dexterity is an acquisition of the utmost consequence. The discrepancies that actually obtain in the physical organisation of the various races of men, are seldom very considerable; and yet, how vast is the difference, in other points of view, between an Indian of Mexico and an Englishman or a Frenchman. The former, ignorant and uninstructed, is poor and miserable, though placed in a country blessed with a soil of exhaustless fertility and a genial climate; the latter, intelligent and educated, is wealthy, prosperous and happy, though placed under comparatively unfavourable circumstances. . . . An ignorant and under-educated

[1] *Op. cit.*, vol. i, pp. 264–5.

people, though possessed of all the materials and powers necessary for the production of wealth, are uniformly sunk in poverty and barbarism.'[1]

4. NEIGHBOURHOOD EFFECTS

It is unnecessary to multiply examples of an attitude which by the end of the classical period had become wellnigh universal. The pioneer effort of Nicholson to measure the magnitude of the human factor in the National Capital, which appears in the first number of the *Economic Journal*, does not argue the question whether investment of this sort is justified, although it devotes some space to the semantic question whether the result should or should not be classified as Capital Wealth. But it is worth while making more explicit wherein the gain was supposed to consist.

The passage from Adam Smith which has already been quoted seems to associate the return to investment in human beings directly with the improved productivity of the individual in the business in which he engages. And this clearly is the sense in which the term is used if we are thinking of parental investment; it is the sense in which it is used again and again in the literature. It covers the return to the individual both of general and specialised ability in so far as this is to be attributed to resources invested in education and training; and it can be conceived to be the difference between what, other things being equal, the individual earns as a result of such investment and what he could have earned without it.

But there is a further sense in which investment of this sort can be said to be productive: the sense, namely, which refers to the increased efficiency of a working population in which adaptability and resourcefulness are promoted by the existence of good standards of education. A community in which there is a rapid

[1] J. R. McCulloch, *Principles of Political Economy*, New ed. (1843) pp. 117–18.

communication of ideas due to common habits of understanding, and high potential mobility due to widespread training of general intelligence, is likely to be more productive absolutely and more capable of development than a community, otherwise similarly situated, in which such standards do not prevail. These are the so-called neighbourhood effects of educational investment; and although they are obviously much more difficult to identify and to measure than the private effects thereof, it is to miss an important part of the picture to ignore their existence. Other things being equal, the difference in productivity per head between a society whose members have a good minimum standard of general education and an uneducated society of the same size is likely to be greater than the figure which would be reached by the same degree of investment in any one representative member, the other members remaining uneducated.

It was doubtless partly with this sort of consideration in mind that, in the section of his book dealing with the duties of the sovereign, Adam Smith was led to urge so strongly the case for minimum standards of education among the great body of the people in societies practising advanced division of labour: 'In the progress of the division of labour, the employment of the far greater part of those who live by labour, that is, of the great body of the people, comes to be confined to a few very simple operations; frequently to one or two. But the understandings of the greater part of men are necessarily formed by their ordinary employments. The man whose whole life is spent in performing a few simple operations, of which the effects too are, perhaps, always the same, or very nearly the same, has no occasion to exert his understanding, or to exercise his invention in finding out expedients for removing difficulties which never occur. He naturally loses, therefore, the habit of such exertion, and generally becomes as stupid and ignorant as it is possible for a human creature to become. The torpor of his mind renders him, not only incapable of relishing or bearing a part in any rational conversation, but of conceiving any generous, noble or tender sentiment, and consequently of forming any just judgment concerning many even of the ordinary duties of private life. Of the great and extensive interests of his country he is altogether incapable of judging; and unless very particular pains have been taken to render him otherwise, he is equally incapable of defending his country in war. The uniformity of his stationary life naturally corrupts the courage of his mind, and makes him regard with abhorrence the irregular, uncertain, and adventurous life of a soldier. It corrupts even the activity of his body, and renders him incapable of exerting his strength with vigour and perseverance, in any other employment than that to which he has been bred. His dexterity at his own particular trade seems, in this manner to be acquired at the expense of his intellectual, social, and martial virtues. But in every improved and civilized society this is the state into which the labouring poor, that is, the great body of the people, must necessarily fall, unless government takes some pains to prevent it.'[1] This, Smith thinks, can be done: reading, writing and accounting 'can be acquired at so early a period of life, that the greater part even of those bred to the lowest occupations have time to acquire them before they can be employed in these occupations. For a very small expense the public can facilitate, can encourage, and can even impose upon the whole body of the people, the necessity of acquiring these most essential parts of education.'[2]

James Mill repeated this argument with explicit reference to Adam Smith in his article on Education in the famous Supplement to the fourth edition of the *Encyclopaedia Britannica*, in which so much of second-generation classical political economy was set

[1] Smith, *The Wealth of Nations*, vol. ii, pp. 267–8.
[2] Ibid., p. 270. It has sometimes been suggested that the attitude here expressed to the more general effects of the division of labour involves a 'contradiction' with what Smith has said earlier on the benefits thereof. This seems to me to be a complete mare's nest. There is no contradiction between the view that repetitive work may involve increased 'dexterity' in that job at the same time as it leads to a narrowness of outlook and, unless offset by other interests, a general numbing of intelligence. This is well argued by Dr Nathan Rosenberg in an excellent article: 'Adam Smith on the Division of Labour: Two Views or One?', *Economica*, n.s., vol. xxxii, no. 126 (May 1965).

forth; and thenceforward emphasis on the importance of education for the maintenance and advancement of the potential of the working population can be regarded as an accepted feature of the main tradition of economic thought, though we have to wait for Marshall's *Principles*[1] for a full and systematic discussion of its various aspects.

5.   THE STATE IN RELATION TO EDUCATION

But how was it to be ensured?   Adam Smith's argument involved two conceptions: the public could 'facilitate' its acquisition, it could also 'even impose' the necessity of elementary education. Facilitation could be brought about 'by establishing in every parish or district a little school where children may be taught for a reward so moderate that even a common labourer may afford it; the master being partly, but not wholly, paid by the public; because, if he were wholly or principally paid by it, he would soon learn to neglect his business'.   Imposition could take place 'by obliging every man to undergo an examination or probation' 'in the most essential parts of education' 'before he can obtain the freedom in any corporation, or be allowed to set up in any trade either in a village or town corporate'.[2]   In this exposition, facilitation by means of provision comes first, imposition by means of the requirement of examination quite definitely second: indeed, stylistically it seems something of an afterthought — if you want to impose standards this is the best way to do it.

By the middle of the nineteenth century the emphasis has altered.   If we turn to Nassau Senior who of all the classical economists paid greatest attention to educational problems, the idea of imposition comes first, in virtue of the child's right to be educated; and facilitation follows because, for the time being at any rate, the poorer classes are said not to be in a position to

[1] *Op. cit.* bk. IV, chs. v, vi.   [2] *Op. cit.* vol. ii, p. 270.

afford the purchase for themselves. The resolutions which he submitted to his colleagues on the Education Commission of the sixties and reproduced in his *Suggestions on Popular Education* set this out very boldly and are worth producing in full:

'1) That the object of society is to protect individuals from wrong.

2) That those who cannot protect themselves are as much entitled to protection as those who can.

3) That children are as much entitled to protection as adults.

4) That education is as much necessary to a child as food is.

5) That it is as much the duty of a parent to educate his child as it is to feed it.

6) That a child is as much wronged by being left uneducated, as it is by being left unfed.

7) That it is as much the duty of the community to see that the child is educated as it is to see that it is fed.

8) That unless the community can and will compel the parent to feed the child, or to educate the child, the community must do so.

9) That the elementary education of a child costs not less than 30s. a year.

10) That there is no reason to believe that now, or at any time that can be defined, that sum is or will be obtainable from the parent.

11) That it is the duty of the State to aid private benevolence in supplying the sum that is not obtainable from the parent.

12) That we ought to recommend a system of State assistance for that purpose.' [1]

It should be added, however, that so far as provision by the State was concerned, Senior hoped that it would not always be necessary. In his Utopia the citizens had acquired middle-class habits and middle-class responsibility; hence it might be hoped that the necessity for subsidy would eventually cease. He was clear, however, that this day was still very far distant: for his generation such assistance was necessary.

For John Stuart Mill, however, the position was not so simple.

[1] N. W. Senior, *Suggestions on Popular Education* (1861) p. 102.

In the *Principles* he laid it down that the government was entitled 'to impose on parents the legal obligation of giving elementary instruction to children' and further that, because of the insufficiency of wages and charitable provision, it was 'the duty of the government to supply the defect by giving pecuniary support to elementary schools, such as to render them accessible to all the children of the poor, either freely or for a payment too inconsiderable to be sensibly felt'.[1] But in the essay *On Liberty*, which was written later, he seems somewhat to have shifted his view. He is still clear about the legal obligation on parents to have their children educated: 'It still remains unrecognized, that to bring a child into existence without a fair prospect of being able, not only to provide food for its body, but instruction and training for its mind, is a moral crime, both against the unfortunate offspring and against society; and that if the parent does not fulfil this obligation, the State ought to see it fulfilled at the charge, as far as possible, of the parent.'

But he no longer emphasises the duty of supporting schools, as distinct from poor students. On the contrary, he goes out of his way to emphasise the dangers of exclusive supply of education by the State: 'If the government would make up its mind to *require* for every child a good education, it might save itself the trouble of *providing* one. It might leave to parents to obtain the education where and how they pleased, and content itself with helping to pay the school fees of the poorer classes of children, and defraying the entire school expenses of those who have no-one else to pay for them. The objections which are argued with reason against State education do not apply to the enforcement of education by the State, but to the State's taking upon itself to direct that education; which is a totally different thing. That the whole or any large part of the education of the people should be in State hands, I go as far as any one in deprecating. All that has been said of the importance of individuality of character, and diversity of opinions and modes of conduct, involves, as of the same unspeakable importance, diversity of education. A general State education is a

[1] *Op. cit.*, pp. 947–50.

mere contrivance for moulding people to be exactly like one another: and as the mould in which it casts them is that which pleases the predominant power in the government, whether this be a monarch, a priesthood, an aristocracy, or the majority of the existing generation; in proportion as it is efficient and successful, it establishes a despotism over the mind, leading by natural tendency to one over the body. An education established and controlled by the State should only exist, if it exist at all, as one among many competing experiments, carried on for the purpose of example and stimulus, to keep the others up to a certain standard of excellence. Unless, indeed, when society in general is in so backward a state that it could or would not provide for itself any proper institutions of education unless the government undertook the task: then, indeed, the government may, as the less of two great evils, take upon itself the business of schools and universities, as it may that of joint-stock companies, when private enterprise, in a shape fitted for undertaking great works of industry, does not exist in the country. But in general, if the country contains a sufficient number of persons qualified to provide education under government auspices, the same persons would be able to and willing to give an equally good education on the voluntary principle, under the assurance of remuneration afforded by a law rendering education compulsory, combined with State aid to those unable to defray the expense.'[1]

Mill's thought in this respect has not influenced action. The concept of support for persons rather than institutions has not been adopted as a governing principle. Nor have his apprehensions of a universal state system been widely shared. But in an age when the very good idea of eliminating selection at an early age in the state system by the creation of comprehensive schools is being made the pretext in certain quarters for a movement to abolish all other types of schooling, his attitude is not altogether without contemporary relevance.

[1] Mill, *On Liberty* (1859) pp. 189–191.

6. THE ADVANCEMENT OF KNOWLEDGE:
BACON TO BENTHAM

Education presumes knowledge to be imparted. This is so whether it takes place in the home, in educational institutions or in the routine business of life. And although it is conceptually inappropriate to speak of knowledge in quantitative terms, it is clear that differences in the range of knowledge available are among the most significant of all influences in determining differences of production per head and hence of different degrees of economic development. In the last analysis the difference between the economic potential of the Stone Age and of the twentieth century is a difference of range of relevant technique and information.

It is a nice question to what extent this has been sufficiently realised in the economic thought of the past. In his *Review of Economic Theory*, Edwin Cannan dwells at some length upon 'the neglect of knowledge' in the classical system and elsewhere. He attributes this partly to a shrinking from platitude, partly to a certain peculiarity in the treatment of the subject by Adam Smith — of which more later — and partly to the fact that knowledge is often a free good and 'economists have generally been inclined to neglect things of no value, however important they may be'.[1] He cited McCulloch and Senior as examples of this frame of mind.

It is possible to admit the indictment as regards emphasis in the formal framework of exposition but yet to feel that the picture is somewhat one-sided. It is just not true that the economic thought of the past was unaware of the relevance to development of technical or other forms of knowledge or that there is lacking in the literature conspicuous emphasis on its importance.

In this connection we may well begin with Bacon. For whatever may be the verdict on his methodology, his conception of the purpose and promise of our knowledge of nature has been a leading influence on progressive thought ever since it was first elaborated;

[1] *Op. cit.* (1929) pp. 122–5.

and its influence on the background of the classical economists is especially relevant in this connection. According to aphorism lxxxi of book I of the *Novum Organum*, 'the true and lawful goal of the sciences is this: that human life be endowed with new discoveries and powers',[1] and in the final section of the same book, the results of such discoveries are the subject of one of its most eloquent passages: 'It remains for me', says the author, 'to say a few words touching the excellency of the end in view. Had they been uttered earlier, they might have seemed like idle wishes; but now that hopes have been raised and unfair prejudices removed, they may perhaps have greater weight. Also if I had finished all myself, and had no occasion to call in others to help and take part in the work, I should even now have abstained from such language, lest it might be taken as a proclamation of my own deserts. But since I want to quicken the industry and rouse and kindle the zeal of others, it is fitting that I put men in mind of some things.

'In the first place then, the introduction of famous discoveries appears to hold by far the first place among human actions; and this was the judgment of the former ages. For to the authors of inventions they awarded divine honours; while to those who did good service in the state (such as founders of cities and empires, legislators, saviours of their country from long endured evils, quellers of tyrannies, and the like) they decreed no higher honours than heroic. And certainly if a man rightly compare the two, he will find that this judgment of antiquity was just. For the benefits of discoveries may extend to the whole race of man, civil benefits only to particular places; the latter last not beyond a few ages, the former through all time. Moreover the reformation of a state in civil matters is seldom brought in without violence and confusion; but discoveries carry blessings with them, and confer benefits without causing harm or sorrow to any.

'Again, discoveries are as it were new creations, and imitations of God's works; as well sang the poet : —

1 *The Philosophical Works of Francis Bacon*, reprinted from the texts and translations of Ellis and Spedding (1905) p. 280.

'To man's frail race great Athens long ago
First gave the seed whence waving harvests grow,
And *re-created* all our life below'

[Lucretius, vi, 1–3]

'And it appears worthy of remark in Solomon, that though mighty in empire and in gold; in the magnificence of his works, his court, his household, and his fleet, in the lustre of his name and the worship of mankind; yet he took none of these to glory in, but pronounced that 'The glory of God is to conceal a thing; the glory of the king to search it out.' [Prov. xxv. 2.]

'Again, let a man only consider what a difference there is between the life of men in the most civilized province of Europe, and in the wildest and most barbarous districts of New India; he will feel it be great enough to justify the saying that "man is a god to man", not only in regard of aid and benefit, but also by a comparison of condition. And this difference comes not from soil, not from climate, not from race, but from the arts.

'Again, it is well to observe the force and virtue and consequences of discoveries; and these are to be seen nowhere more conspicuously than in those three which were unknown to the ancients, and of which the origin, though recent, is obscure and inglorious; namely, printing, gunpowder and the magnet. For these three have changed the whole face and state of things throughout the world; the first in literature, the second in warfare, the third in navigation; whence have followed innumerable changes; insomuch that no empire, no sect, no star seems to have exerted greater power and influence in human affairs than these mechanical discoveries.'[1]

Bacon was a general philosopher and these remarks, powerful as they are, are incidental to a wider view of the status of scientific knowledge in general. The question we have to ask is to what extent was this outlook shared by those who addressed themselves more systematically to the problem of economic development: and here, I submit, the evidence is much more positive than Cannan's strictures would lead us to believe.

[1] Ibid., p. 300.

D

To begin with Adam Smith. It was Cannan's criticism here, not that Smith left out the importance of invention but that he subsumed it under a general view of the advantages of the division of labour. This is true enough. But since in the Smithian system these advantages are one of the two influences on the level of production per head, it would surely be misleading to deny one of their main constituents an important place in the analysis. In a footnote to the critical passage in his edition of *The Wealth of Nations*, Cannan himself draws attention to forceful illustrations of these advantages which appear in the Glasgow *Lectures*: 'Two men and three horses will do more in a day with the plough than twenty men without it. The miller and his servant will do more with the water mill than a dozen with the hand mill, though it too be a machine.'[1] The fact that in *The Wealth of Nations* itself the author omitted these on the ground that 'everybody must be sensible how much labour is facilitated and abridged by the application of proper machinery' does not indicate any underestimate of their importance. The worst that can be said of it is that it suffers from a certain deficiency of emphasis.

No such strictures could be passed upon the utterances in this connection of the next great figure in the history of social thought, Jeremy Bentham. In an incautious moment Adam Smith had allowed himself to say that if the rate of interest had no legal upper limit, the levels which would prevail would mean that none but prodigals and projectors would obtain free Capital; and in his famous *Defence of Usury* Bentham attacks this position. His last chapter is devoted to the vindication of projectors, those who put into practice innovations in technique; and the importance of this process could hardly be more strongly emphasised. He begs of Adam Smith to reflect 'Whether whatever is now the routine of trade was not at its commencement, *project*, whether whatever is now *establishment*, was not at one time innovation?' and reproaches him for condemning as 'rash and ill-grounded, all those projects by which our species have been successively advanced

[1] Smith, *Lectures on Justice, Police, Revenue, and Arms*, ed. Cannan (1896) p. 167.

from that state in which acorns were their food and raw hides their clothing to the state in which it stands at present.'[1] At a later stage in the argument, he invokes the existence of 'so numerous and respectable a body of men, . . . the members of the Society for the Encouragement of the Arts'; and observing that 'of that popular institution, the very professed and capital object is the encouragement which you commend as fit exercise for the arm of power', he urges: 'But if it be right to crush the acting malefactor, it would be downright inconsistency not to crush at the same time, or rather not to begin with crushing, these, their hirers and abettors.'[2, 3]

In the light of these passages it would be hard to complain of any lack of appreciation by Jeremy Bentham of the importance of improvements in technical knowledge.

7. BABBAGE AND RAE

If we turn to the nineteenth century we find this attitude even more articulate. The Baconian attitude to the advancement of

[1] Bentham, *Works*, ed. Bowring (1790), vol. ii, p. 22. The order, of the quotation is reversed.

[2] Ibid., pp. 183–4.

[3] In this connection, I cannot refrain from quoting what must surely be regarded as one of the most successful predictions in applied economics: 'Birmingham and Sheffield are ptiched upon by you as examples, the one of a projecting town, the other of an unprojecting one. Can you forgive my saying, I rather wonder that this comparison of your own chosing, did not suggest some suspicions of the justice of the conceptionsyouhadtakenup,tothedisadvantageof projectors.Sheffielofthe is an old oak : Birmingham, but a mushroom. What if we should find the mushroom still vaster and more vigorous than the oak ? Not but the one as well as the other, at what time soever planted, must equally have been planted by projectors ; for though Tubal Cain himself were to be brought post from Armenia to plant Sheffield, Tubal Cain himself was as arrant a projector in his day, as ever Sir Thomas Lombe was, or bishop Blaise : but Birmingham, it seems, claims in common parlance the title of a projecting town, to the exclusion of the other, the spirit of project smells fresher and stronger there than elsewhere.' Ibid., pp. 27–8.

knowledge was dominant in a wide variety of circles from the sober hierarchs of the *Edinburgh Review* to the wilder fanatics of continental social thought — it would be difficult to find a more extravagant estimate of what scientists can give to mankind than the underlying outlook of Saint-Simon's *Lettres d'un habitant de Genève*. The Industrial Revolution was beginning to transform the conditions of economic activity; and recognition of its sources in speculative thought and practical invention became more and more general.

We may first quote two examples from literature which was not specifically in the English classical tradition, in the stricter interpretation of that term.

First the widely read and widely praised *On the Economy of Machinery and Manufacture* by Charles Babbage, Lucasian Professor of Mathematics at Cambridge from 1828 to 1839 and pioneer of the computing machine. This work, which ran into four editions, was designed to explain 'The accumulation of skill and science which has been directed to diminish the difficulty of producing manufactured goods';[1] and after the most extensive review of the leading technological features of contemporary manufacture and their economic implications, the conclusion is that 'it is impossible not to perceive that the arts and manufactures of the country are intimately connected with the progress of the severer sciences: and that as we advance in the career of improvement, every step requires, for its success that this question should be rendered more intimate.'

'The applied sciences', he goes on to argue, 'derive their facts from experiment; but the reasonings, on which their chief utility depends, are the province of what is called abstract Science. It has been shown, that the division of labour is no less applicable to mental productions than to those in which material bodies are concerned; and it follows, that the efforts for the improvement of its manufactures which any country can make with the greatest probability of success, must arise from the combined exertions of all those most skilled in the theory, as well as in the practice of the

[1] *Op. cit.*, 4th ed. (1835) pp. 3-4.

arts; each labouring in that department for which his natural capacity and acquired habits have rendered him most fit.'[1]

As a second opinion, we may quote John Rae, as obscure as Babbage was well known, but for all that, probably the most profound of all who have treated of this subject. The remarkable chapter on invention in the *New Principles of Political Economy* opens thus: 'Invention is the most important of the secondary agents, to the influence of which man is subject. To us it is the great immediate maker of almost all that is the subject of our thoughts, or ministers to our enjoyments, or necessities, nor is there any portion of our existence, which is not indebted to its antecedent forming power. Wherever it really is, it is recognised as one and the same, by this its formative capacity. It is always a maker, and, in a double sense, a maker. From the depths of the infinity lying within and without us, it brings visibly before us forms previously hidden. These are its first works. But neither does it intend to stop, nor does it, in fact, stop here. The forms which its eye thus catches, and its skill "bodies forth" into material shape, pass not away; they remain. Things of power, true workers, drawing to themselves, and fashioning to their semblance, the changeable and fleeting crowd that time hurries down its stream, they are, in truth, the only permanent dwellers in the world, and rulers of it.'[2] It would be difficult to argue that the author of such a passage did not, to use Cannan's words, give 'knowledge the prominent place which it should have occupied'.

8. THE PLACE OF KNOWLEDGE IN THE CLASSICAL THEORY

Cannan's judgment, occurring as it does in a work devoted to a review of economic thought in general, certainly fails over a substantial part of the field. But the main target, as exemplified by

[1] Ibid., p. 379.   [2] *Op. cit.*, p. 208.

the citations of Senior and McCulloch, is nineteenth-century classical economics; and here it is not to be denied that there is a certain case to be examined.

At the same time, on any calm view, it must be said that there is a certain implausibility about any statement which would suggest that in their general outlook on the forces making for development, the nineteenth-century classical writers were indifferent to the growth of knowledge and the progress of invention. The air was full of exhortations to the working classes to appreciate these influences and to do nothing to impede their operation; and James Mill, at least, was a member of the committee of the Society for the Diffusion of Useful Knowledge which made systematic attempts to organise such propaganda. One of its most famous publications was Charles Knight's *The Results of Machinery* (1830),[1] a veritable psalm of David to the benefits of invention, which in later editions was incorporated by its author in a work actually entitled *Knowledge is Power*. A similar attitude is displayed in the *Outlines of Social Economy* by William Ellis whom we know to have worked intimately with John Stuart Mill;[2] and the many tales of Harriet Martineau are intended to point the same moral.

But Cannan's attack was focused on the central literature: and here at first glance there is some justification for his strictures. They would miss the point if directed against Ricardo; for as we have seen, Ricardo was concerned with value and distribution and

---

[1] At first published with no indication of authorship by Charles Knight, Pall Mall East 18. According to Foxwell, who was usually so accurate, this work was 'usually assumed' to have been written by Brougham, who was President of the Society. (Introduction to the translation of Anton Menger's *Right to the whole Produce of Labour* (1899).) But there can be no real doubt that the author was Charles Knight, who says so in the introduction to the later work quoted above (*Knowledge is Power* (1855) p. 3). When I drew up the footnote referring to *The Results of Machinery* on p. 134 of my *Theory of Economic Policy*, I was ignorant of this later work and so adopted Foxwell's statement of the usual assumptions. I was only disabused of this by an accidental purchase of *Knowledge is Power*.

[2] *Op. cit.* (1846) pp. 49–52.

expressly repudiated capacity to deal in any helpful way with production. But it is true that there is no mention of knowledge by Mc-
Culloch or Senior in their formal statements of the influences determining the level of production. Cannan certainly makes a point here.

At the same time it must be said that other pronouncements by
the two writers in question indicate without the possibility of
contradiction a full awareness of this factor and its great importance.

Thus McCulloch, reviewing Babbage in the *Edinburgh Review*
for June 1833, delivers himself, with characteristic heaviness, as
follows: 'Civilized man is, in fact, indebted to tools and machines,
not for an increase of power merely, but for almost everything that
he possesses. Perhaps not one in a thousand of the arts practised
amongst us could be carried on by the hand only. Those who
investigate the history of the human race, who trace their slow
and gradual progress from their lowest and most abject to their
highest and most polished state, will find that it has always been
accompanied and chiefly promoted by the invention and improvement of tools and engines. What, we ask, has falsified all the
predictions of Hume and Smith, as to the increase of the public
debt, and enables us to support without difficulty a load of taxes
that would have crushed our fathers, as it would crush any other
people? This wonderful result has not assuredly been owing to
any peculiar sagacity on the part of our rulers, nor to the miserable
quackery of sinking funds, custom-house regulations, and such
like devices. There cannot, indeed, be the shadow of a doubt that
it is to be wholly ascribed to the stupendous inventions and discoveries of Hargreaves, Arkwright, Watt, Wedgewood, Crompton,
Cartwright and a few others. These added so prodigiously to
our capacities of production, that we went on rapidly increasing
in population and wealth, notwithstanding an expenditure of
blood and treasure unparalleled in the history of the world. It is
believed that an individual can at this moment, by means of the
improved machinery now in use, produce about 200 times the
quantity of cotton goods that an individual could have produced
at the accession of George III in 1760! The improvement in
other branches, though for the most part less striking than in the

cotton manufacture, is still very great; and in some, as in the lace manufacture, it is little if at all inferior. The high and conspicuous place we occupy among the nations of the earth, is not owing to our possessing a greater population, a finer climate, or a more fertile soil; but to the superior art we have evinced in availing ourselves of the powers of nature. This has multiplied our resources, and increased our power in a degree that was not previously conceivable. It is not going too far to say that we have, at the very least, derived ten times more advantage from the spinning-jenny and the steam-engine, than from all our conquests in India, though these have added nearly 100 millions of subjects to our empire.'

Similarly Senior, in the manuscripts of his lectures delivered in Oxford in 1848–9, as published in S. L. Levy's deplorable conflation, pronounces with equal emphasis: 'It is scarcely necessary to do more than allude to the influence on wealth of intellectual cultivation. During the last one hundred years the wealth of England has more than quadrupled. We are not more diligent, or more frugal than our grandfathers — perhaps we are rather less so. We have not enjoyed peculiar security. At no period of our history have we had foreign wars so long, so destructive, or so dangerous. We have had two great civil wars, one of which ended in the dismemberment of our American empire. And yet such has been our increase in wealth that though our population has more than doubled and, therefore, might be supposed to be less favourably situated with respect to one great productive instrument, the land, there is scarcely a family that could bear to be fed or clothed, or lodged as its great-grandfather was in 1764. By far the greater part of this marvelous increase of wealth is owing to a still more marvelous increase of knowledge.'[1]

When we come to John Stuart Mill, who must certainly be

---

[1] Nassau W. [*sic*] Senior, *Industrial Efficiency and Social Economy*, ed. S. Leon Levy (1928) vol. i, p. 195. It should be noted in fairness to Cannan that this was not available at the time of publication of his *Review*. The McCulloch article, however, although anonymous, was available in the Goldsmith's Library, in McCulloch's own collection of his contributions to the *Edinburgh Review*.

taken seriously as a repository of the central classical tradition, Cannan does somewhat grudgingly allow that he is 'entitled to some credit' for including knowledge in his five 'Causes of superior productiveness' in the *Principles of Political Economy*; and he quotes one sentence which develops this thought. He does not, however, state that this sentence is followed by more than a page of elucidatory development including citation of Babbage and an explanation that machinery is 'far from being the only mode in which the effects of knowledge in aiding production are exemplified'.[1] Nor does he cite the much more exciting passage in the chapter on the 'Grounds and Limits of the *Laissez-Faire* Principle' in which Mill argues for the provision of modes 'of insuring to the public the services of scientific discoveries, and perhaps of some other classes of savants, by affording them the means of support consistently with devoting a sufficient portion of time to their peculiar pursuits', and goes on to recommend university fellowships and chairs as the most suitable instruments for the purpose.[2]

Most surprisingly, after citing Mill, Cannan goes on to say that 'Later writers have failed to develop the subject.' But this is simply wrong. There are two excellent chapters on invention in Hearn's *Plutology*, rightly praised by Sir Arnold Plant in his well-known article on Patents. And, not to prolong a difference of opinion with a great scholar whose works are too apt to be under-valued nowadays, I will conclude by a citation which I certainly should have expected Cannan to have remembered.

'. . . mental faculties, like manual dexterity, die with those who possess them', wrote Marshall, 'but the improvement which each generation contributes to the machinery of manufacture or to the organon of science is handed down to the next. There may be no abler sculptors now than those who worked on the Parthenon, no thinker with more mother-wit than Aristotle. But the appliances of thought develop cumulatively as do those of material production.

'Ideas, whether those of art and science, or those embodied in

[1] Mill, *op. cit.*, vol. i, p. 107.   [2] Ibid., pp. 968–9.

D 2

practical appliances, are the most "real" of the gifts that each generation receives from its predecessors. The world's material wealth would quickly be replaced if it were destroyed, but the ideas by which it was made were retained. If however, the ideas were lost, but not the material wealth, then that would dwindle and the world would go back to poverty. And most of our knowledge of mere facts could quickly be recovered if it were lost, but the constructive ideas of thought remained; while if the ideas perished, the world would enter again on the Dark Ages.'[1]

After this surely there is little that need be said to emphasise the significance of knowledge to the processes of economic development.

[1] Marshall, *Principles of Economics*, pp. 779–80.

ORGANISATION AND POLICY

I. INTRODUCTORY

THE last three lectures have considered the conditions of development from a somewhat mechanical point of view. I have been tracing the history of thought concerning the significance for the growth of average income of numbers, of accumulation, and of education and technical knowledge. But this does not in itself provide a history of thought regarding the activating and organising influences in this connection; and it is to this subject that I now turn. I wish to make a broad survey of the history of theories of organisation and policy in regard to economic development. What views have influenced serious speculation on the appropriate pattern of institutions and initiative? With a subject of this kind you will well understand, I hope, that my treatment must be even more confined to salient features and tendencies than in the three preceding lectures.

2. THE POLICIES OF MERCANTILISM

As I said in the first lecture, there are no theories of development as such in the literature of the mercantilist period: there are only suggestions for particular acts of policy. From the point of view of this survey they fall into two groups.

First come recommendations regarding enterprises and activities which, in the nature of things, can only be carried out by the state or as a result of specific state authorisation: road construction, the building of docks and bridges, land reclamation, the construction of canals. Some of these proposals are argued with considerable force and cogency and their relevance to the general development of the economy is brought out clearly. But there is nothing in their nature or their justification to distinguish them from other such proposals made at other periods of history. They could all be perfectly well classified under Adam Smith's third type of 'duties of the sovereign' — 'the duty of erecting and maintaining certain public works and certain public institutions, which it can never be for the interest of any individual or small number of individuals, to erect and maintain; because the profit could never repay the expence to any individual or small number of individuals, though it may frequently do much more than repay it to a great society'.[1]

Secondly came proposals for fostering or promoting the growth of particular branches of industry which in the absence of such intervention would develop differently or not at all. Such recommendations are the special characteristic of the mercantilist literature, using that phrase in its wide sense. Many of them are designed to promote a favourable balance of trade; such proposals fall under the heading of mercantilism in the narrower sense. But many are designed simply to promote the growth of the industries favoured, as if there were some virtue *per se* in having a prosperous wool industry — just as at the present day the governments of various under-developed countries act as if there were inevitable advantage in having refineries or steel mills, regardless of what their profitability would be in the absence of special encouragement. And it is the characteristic of all such recommendations that they tend to be made for every kind of reason other than a consideration of whether the use of resources in this way rather than in some other way will tend to add more to the annual produce of the community: and it is taken for granted that, unless there is paternalistic guidance of the enterprise of the individual, the evolution of the system is likely to be unsatisfactory. Thus the redoubtable Samuel Fortrey, whose *England's Interest and Improve-*

[1] Smith, *The Wealth of Nations*, vol. ii, p. 185.

ment is devoted *inter alia* to a diatribe against trade with France, emphasises 'how necessary it is that the public profits should be in a single power to direct whose interest is only the benefit of the whole'.[1] A revealing picture of the general outlook of this literature is provided by the famous tract of von Hornick, *Oesterreich über alles, wann es nur will* (Austria over all if she only will).

3. THE ANTI-MERCANTILIST PROTEST

It was against this type of thought that the great eighteenth-century liberal thinkers raised their protests. The Physiocrats in France and David Hume and Adam Smith in Britain found this philosophy of *ad hoc* interventions intolerable, and directed withering criticism against both the underlying attitude and its manifestation in particular measures. If we may take Adam Smith as the leading representative of this movement, we find that, considered in regard to the theory of development, his protest has two principal aspects.

It was a protest, first against what he regarded as a misuse of resources. This comes out particularly clearly in his analysis of the effects of bounties. At an earlier stage he had laid down the criteria by which he proposed to judge all such measures. 'According as they tend either to increase or diminish the value of this annual produce, they must evidently tend either to increase or diminish the real wealth and revenue of the country.'[2] Now, considering bounties, he applies these criteria as follows: 'The trades, it is to be observed, which are carried on by means of bounties, are the only ones which can be carried on between two nations for any considerable time together, in such a manner as that one of them shall always and regularly lose, or sell its goods for less than it really costs to send them to market. But if the

[1] Reprinted in McCulloch, *Select Collection of Early English Tracts on Commerce* (1856) p. 219.

[2] Smith, *op. cit.*, vol. i, p. 417.

bounty did not repay to the merchant what he would otherwise lose upon the price of his goods, his own interest would soon oblige him to employ his stock in another way, or to find out a trade in which the price of the goods would replace to him, with the ordinary profit, the capital employed in sending them to market. The effect of bounties, like that of all the expedients of the mercantile system, can only be to force the trade of a country into a channel much less advantageous than that on which it would naturally run of its own accord.'[1] It is clear, is it not, that here in a primitive form you have the fundamental idea of the opportunity cost test of allocative efficiency?

But beyond this it was a protest against the assumption of centralised wisdom. The attitude of mind which Adam Smith was attacking was apt to take it for granted that the princes and the governments of the world had — or could have — knowledge which would enable them to decide where productive effort was best applied and how development of productive power could best be organised. And for this attitude Smith had the profoundest contempt. He had theoretical grounds for believing that society was better served by decentralised initiative — I shall be speaking of these in a moment — and he obviously felt that no inkling of these had ever penetrated the heads of his opponents. And, as an historian and a man of the world with wide practical contacts, he had — or fancied that he had — solid grounds for thinking that this assumption of disinterested centralised wisdom realised itself in practice in a mass of blundering inefficiency and the ascendancy of the sinister interest of the pressure groups. 'The statesman', he said, 'who should attempt to direct private people in what manner they ought to employ their capitals, would not only load himself with a most unnecessary attention, but assume an authority which could be safely trusted not only to no single person, but to no council or senate whatever, and which would no-where be so dangerous as in the hands of a man who had folly and presumption enough to fancy himself fit to exercise it.'[2]

[1] Ibid., vol. i, p. 8.   [2] Ibid., p. 421.

He was moreover likely to be influenced by interested persons. Advice on policy of this sort was likely to come from groups of dealers and producers: 'the proposal of any new law or regulation of commerce which comes from this order, ought always to be listened to with great precaution, and ought never to be adopted till after having been long and carefully examined, not only with the most scrupulous, but with the most suspicious attention. It comes from an order of men, whose interest is never exactly the same with that of the public, who have generally an interest to deceive and even to oppress the public, and who accordingly have, upon many occasions, both deceived and oppressed it.'[1]

4. THE SYSTEM OF NATURAL LIBERTY

The critique of mercantilism from this point of view was therefore clear. It was a drag on the best use of resources and an unwarrantable assumption of superior knowledge on the part of monarchs or elected persons. It was also liable to be influenced by sinister pressures. But to establish a case that this kind of intervention must stop, it was necessary not only to show that it worked badly but also that if it did not take place, there would still be order and development; that in the absence of central guidance and control, there would nevertheless not be chaos but, on the contrary, a system which sustained and directed the division of labour and provided an incentive to accumulation and progress. This was the famous system of natural liberty of Adam Smith.

As I hope you all know, the background to this system was a framework of law and order. Contrary to beliefs fostered even to this day by ignorance or the sophistry of popular propaganda, it involved no assumption that the unregulated play of self-interest and self-preservation would lead to orderly arrangements. The system of natural liberty was emphatically not a Hobbesian state of nature where, because of mutual enmity and depredation,

[1] Ibid., p. 250.

anarchy and chaos prevailed.   On the contrary, it assumed a strong state and a body of law restraining antisocial behaviour and prescribing an elaborate code of rules relating to property and contract.   And in the British version, as opposed to that presented by the Physiocrats, this code was conceived, not as some simple and rigid deduction from imaginary principles of natural law and natural rights, but rather as an historically evolving *organism* subject to continued revision and improvement in the light of considerations of utility.   There is no time in this context to elaborate on this theme.   But to those who have any doubts, I would refer to the classic discussion of justice and property in David Hume's *Enquiry Concerning the Principles of Morals*.   It assumed, too, as we shall see, positive functions of the state where the interest of private individuals was unlikely to be effective.

Within this framework, Smith argued, the force of self-interest combined with the existence of markets could be trusted without central guidance to secure a division of labour involving a use of resources tending continually, where not obstructed, to produce the goods and services which were the subject of the most urgent effective demand and at the same time to provoke a continual search for means of improvement.

Thus the opportunity for exchange made possible the division of labour: a man could specialise as a producer knowing that, as a consumer, he could meet his varied wants by the proceeds of the sale of his products.   Working with the intention of supplying his own and his family's needs, he could count on the availability of products brought into being by others inspired by like motives. 'It is not from the benevolence of the butcher, the brewer, or the baker, that we expect our dinner but from their regard to their own interest.   We address ourselves, not to their humanity but to their self-love, and never talk to them of our own necessities but of their advantages.'[1]

The self-interest thus evoked was guided by the operation of the market.   Prices from day to day were governed by the inter-play of demand expressed in money and the supplies available.   If

[1] Smith, *The Wealth of Nations*, vol. i, p. 16.

a price thus determined offered exceptional prospects of gain in relation to costs of production, there was an incentive for more production of the product involved; if it involved losses the incentive worked in the opposite direction. Thus there was continual pressure so to direct activities that the individual contribution to the annual produce was of the greatest value — the famous invisible hand which guided the producer 'to promote an end which was no part of his intention'.[1] And it should be noted, especially in regard to the subject matter of this lecture, that this function of the market was conceived quite as much in a dynamic as a statistical sense. Much of the more technical development of the analysis of value and distribution has concentrated on precise formulation of the conditions of a stationary equilibrium. But this is not the conception of *The Wealth of Nations*. The division of labour itself is conceived to give birth to invention and improvement; and the force of self-interest, always seeking greater gain, disturbs existing equilibria, if opportunity for such gain presents itself.

This indeed is the whole spirit of the Smithian conception; and, if we turn back to the discussion of bounties we find that it is explicitly contrasted with the spirit of mercantilism as Smith conceived it: 'That system of laws . . . which is connected with the establishment of the bounty, seems to deserve no part of the praise which has been bestowed upon it. The improvement and prosperity of Great Britain, which has been so often ascribed to those laws, may very easily be accounted for by other causes. That security which the laws in Great Britain give to every man that he shall enjoy the fruits of his own labour, is alone sufficient to make any country flourish, notwithstanding these and twenty other absurd regulations of commerce; and this security was perfected by the revolution much about the same time that the bounty was established. The natural effort of every individual to better his own condition, when suffered to exert itself with freedom and security, is so powerful a principle, that it is alone, and without any assistance, not only capable of carrying on the society to

[1] Ibid., vol. i, p. 421.

wealth and prosperity, but of surmounting a hundred impertinent obstructions with which the folly of human laws too often incumbers its operations. . . .'[1]

5. THE ENTREPRENEUR AND HIS FUNCTIONS

So much for the broad philosophy of the system of economic freedom. I have described it by special reference to Adam Smith's exposition. But it is to get the classical system out of all perspective if it is not realised that thenceforward all this was taken for granted as essential background. The fact that some outstanding figures, such as Ricardo, focused their attention on problems arising within this system, does not mean that they felt their outlook to be in any sense alien to it.

Considered in regard to development, however, there are two aspects of this system where the evolution of thought deserves further notice — aspects relating respectively to the role of the entrepreneur and to that of the joint stock company. I will deal with these in that order.

So far as the entrepreneur is concerned, we must go, not to Adam Smith, but to the incomparable Cantillon. There in that extraordinary essay of his we find a clear-cut statement of the basic conception of the position of the entrepreneural function as it has survived its various vicissitudes down to the present day. Leaving on one side the great landowners, whose tastes determined the main set of the systems he was concerned with, Cantillon divides the active members of society into two groups: those whose incomes are fixed by contract and those whose incomes are in the nature of a residue: 'Except the Prince and the Proprietors of Land, all the inhabitants of a state . . . can be divided into two classes . . . all the undertakers are as it were on unfixed wages and the others on wages fixed so long as they receive them, though their function and ranks may be very unequal. The General who has his pay, the Courtier his pension and the

1 Ibid., vol. ii, pp. 42–3.

Domestic Servant who has wages all fall into this last class. All
the rest are undertakers, whether they set up with a capital to
conduct their enterprise, or are undertakers of their own labour
without capital, and *they may be regarded as living at uncertainty*
(my italics).'[1]

The function of the entrepreneur or risk-taker — as one who
faces the uncertainties of production in anticipation of demand —
was thus early established, as was the fundamental distinction
between contractual and residual incomes. But the function of
innovation as such is not separated out in the literature until much
later when the distinction between statics and dynamics, which
John Stuart Mill took over from Auguste Comte, had become
fashionable. The importance of organising activities and leadership received signal recognition in Saint-Simon's piquant contrast
between the consequences of the disappearance respectively of
monarchs and statesmen and of the heads of business.[2] But there
was no sharp contrast between organisation to meet day-to-day
contingencies and organisation to bring about change. To the
majority of the classical school and other contemporaries, Schumpeter's sharp distinction between innovation and routine management, with the reservation of the title of the entrepreneur for those
concerned in the former type of activity, would have seemed
formalistic and out of touch with reality.

There was, moreover, a divergence of conceptions as regards
the identity of the entrepreneur, particularly in regard to the
receipt of profits. Cantillon's conception embraced those who
owned capital and those who did not; and this clearly harmonises
with accounting practice from that day to this. But subsequent
analysis, for purposes of the theory of distribution, tended to see
differences of origin within this broad grouping and this led to
differences of emphasis.

Thus for Adam Smith profits — what was left after paying
wages and rent — were essentially the profits *of stock*, the residues

[1] Cantillon, *Essai sur la Nature du Commerce*, p. 55.
[2] *Selected Writings of Henri Comte de Saint-Simon*, ed. Markham
(1952) pp. 72-3.

accruing to those who put their capitals at risk. In so far as these residues differed from the passive incomes of those who advanced capital on a contract basis, they were said to contain an element of 'wages of superintendence'.[1]   But the fundamental source of profit was the employment of capital.   J. B. Say, however, who in many ways is to be regarded as the populariser of Smith, objected to this lumping together, as he thought, of two kinds of income.   For him profit was essentially the reward of the entrepreneur, who in his conception was the organiser and leader and not necessarily the provider of capital.   (It is significant that his translator, C. R. Prinsep, renders the French 'entrepreneur' as 'adventurer'.)   Say emphasised the different analytical significance, as he saw it, between this type of income and the return to capital.

From this divergence there sprang two traditions.   On the whole, continental and American economists, following Say, regarded profit as something due to the very positive activities of someone called the entrepreneur, and profit, as a distributive share, as something to be treated quite separately from business profit in the ordinary sense.   In this tradition come F. A. Walker's treatment of profit as the rent of a special kind of ability, J. B. Clark's conception of profit as a dynamic surplus, and those constructions of Walras, which so upset Edgeworth, of stationary conditions with entrepreneurs who made neither gain nor loss.   Schumpeter's heroic innovators who lose their designation as entrepreneurs if they engage in routine operations are only the final development of this line of evolution.

In contrast to this, the nineteenth-century English classical economists, sticking closer to reality, followed Smith in regarding profits as the residue accruing to those who employed their capitals to set industry in motion.   Apart from the yield of capital, they distinguished elements in this residue which Mill described as 'interest, insurance and wages of superintendence'.[2]   But the term 'profit' was reserved for the residue itself.   In this they were

---

[1] Smith, *The Wealth of Nations*, vol. i, pp. 54-5.
[2] Mill, *Principles of Political Economy*, p. 402.

followed by Marshall. In Marshall there is plenty of reference to the positive activities of entrepreneurship in the continental sense — 'leadership' is one of Marshall's words.[1] But business profits are still treated in the gross sense, any special returns to business skill being treated, within this total, as earnings of management. This usage may be attributed partly to inertia or revulsion from the extreme unreality of the continental tradition. But, by the time of Marshall, the typical form of industrial organisation at least was becoming the joint stock company. There was therefore a good deal to be said for regarding the company as such as the entrepreneur — at least in Cantillon's sense — in which case to continue to call its excess of receipts over expenditure profits, just like that, was not only more in accordance with ordinary business practice, but also more in harmony with the original conception of the entrepreneural function.

6. THE JOINT STOCK PRINCIPLE

This brings me to the joint stock company and the conception of its role in economic development.

Here we have a case where the evolution of thought resulted in a very considerable modification of attitudes. Adam Smith thought poorly of joint stock companies. He passed a very adverse judgment on the record of the great trading companies abroad; and in general, he thought that joint stock companies without exclusive monopolistic privileges were only likely to be successful where 'all the operations [were] capable of being reduced to what is called a routine, or to such uniformity of method as admits of little or no variation'. The only trades where he thought such conditions prevailed were banking, insurance, the making and maintenance of canals and the similar trade of water supply: and even here his approval of such arrangements depended upon the fact that greater capital was required than 'could easily be collected

[1] Marshall, *Principles of Economics*, pp. 298–9.

into a private copartnery'.[1]   For the rest he argued that: 'To
buy in one market, in order to sell, with profit, in another, when
there are many competitors in both; to watch over, not only the
occasional variations in the demand, but the greater and more
frequent variations in the competition, or in the supply which that
demand is likely to get from other people, and to suit with dexterity
and judgement both the quantity and quality of each assortment of
goods to all these circumstances, is a species of warfare of which
the operations are continually changing, and which can scarce
ever be conducted successfully, without such an unremitting
exertion of vigilance and attention, as cannot long be expected
from the directors of a joint stock company.'[2]

Nevertheless, as time went on, the pressure of facts became more
and more adverse to Smith's very radical attitude. The development of technique brought it about that capital was required on a
scale larger than 'could easily be collected into a private copartnery' — to use Smith's phrase — and common sense suggested
that the raising of this capital was likely to be seriously impeded if
the subscribers were liable to the extent of all their property for
the debts of the enterprise in the event of its failure. Hence a
growing demand for the easy grant of incorporation with the privi-
lege of limited liability, which, as is well known, terminated with the
fundamental legislation of 1855 and 1856.

In this controversy the economists were divided. Overstone

---

[1] Smith, *The Wealth of Nations*, vol. ii, pp. 246–7. It is worth noting
Smith's strong distrust of 'joint stock companies, which are established
for the public spirited purpose of promoting some particular manufacture' which he thought 'over and above managing their own affairs
ill, to the diminution of the general stock of the society, can in other
respects scarce ever fail to do more harm than good. Notwithstanding
the most upright intentions the unavoidable partiality of their directors
to particular branches of the manufacture . . . is a real discouragement
to the rest and necessarily breaks, more or less, that natural proportion
which would otherwise establish itself between judicious industry and
profit, and which, to the general industry of the country is of all en-
couragements the greatest and the most effectual.' Ibid., p. 248.

[2] Ibid., p. 245.

and McCulloch were vehement opposers of any such development. McCulloch's fulminations have to be read to be believed. 'In the scheme laid down by Providence for the government of the world', he argued, 'there is no shifting or narrowing of responsibilities, every man being personally answerable for all his actions. But the advocates of limited responsibility proclaim in their superior wisdom that the scheme of Providence may be advantageously modified, and that debts and obligations may be contracted which the debtors, though they have the means, shall not be bound to discharge.'[1] But there were others, equally eminent, who took the opposite view. Senior and G. Ward Norman testified in favour of the principle of limited liability; and in his *Principles* John Stuart Mill lent the weight of his authority against the arguments of its opponents. 'If a number of persons choose to associate for carrying out any operation of commerce or industry, agreeing among themselves and announcing to those with whom they deal that the members of the association do not undertake to be responsible beyond the amount of the subscribed capital,' he asked, 'is there any reason that the law should raise objections to this proceeding, and should impose on them the unlimited responsibility which they disclaim?' His answer was no. 'There seems no more need for interfering with the individual judgement in this sort of transaction, than in any other part of the private business of life.'[2]

At the same time, in an earlier chapter, he had recognised the tendency to substitute large establishments for small ones, a change greatly facilitated by the formation of joint stock companies, and had even committed himself to the statement that 'with a view merely to production, and to the greatest efficiency of labour this change is wholly beneficial'.[3] Adam Smith's strictures, he thought, depended on 'an overstatement of a true principle, often met with in Adam Smith'; he had fixed his observation 'too exclusively on the superior energy and more unremitting

---

[1] McCulloch, 'Partnerships. Limited and Unlimited Liability' in *Encyclopaedia Britannica*, 8th ed., vol. vii, p. 321.

[2] Mill, *op. cit.*, p. 898.   [3] Ibid., vol. i, p. 141.

attention brought to a business in which the whole stake and the whole gain belong to the persons conducting it', to the neglect of countervailing considerations which went far to offset this point of superiority.

Mill was perhaps biased by his hope that, sooner or later, institutions would be evolved depending less on the forces of self-interest than pure individualism: and the joint stock company in some aspects may have seemed a progress in that direction. But recognition of the utility of this method of mobilising capital and so promoting development tended thereafter to become general, even if at the same time there was widespread recognition of the new problems to which it gave rise. To read, for instance, Marshall's discussion of joint stock enterprise in *Industry and Trade*[1] is to realise what a great distance had been traversed since the days of Adam Smith.

7. PUBLIC ENTERPRISE IN A SYSTEM OF ECONOMIC FREEDOM

So much for the salient features of the so-called system of econ-omic freedom conceived as a method of promoting orderly pro-duction and development. Thus presented, however, the system was not without limitations even in the minds of its exponents. I have emphasised already the indispensable background of a framework of law and order authoritatively imposed. But beyond this, there were functions intimately associated with development, where it came to be recognised that unregulated private initiative, either individual or corporative, was not appropriate, for one reason or another. Such for instance was the provision of roads, bridges, harbours, etc.

The characteristic of such undertakings as laid down by Adam Smith was that 'the profit could never repay the expense to any individual or small number of individuals' although 'they might

[1] Marshall, *op. cit.*, (1919) pp. 308–28.

be in the highest degree advantageous to a great society'. This, of course, did not imply that they were beyond the capacity of joint stock enterprise: and in spite of his suspicion of the zeal of such enterprise, Smith was indeed prepared to entrust some such enterprises to this form of organisation; canals, for instance. But, beyond this, there was fear of inappropriate charges which appeared to be especially acute where the roads were concerned: and here, although he deprecated central control, Smith recommended public commissioners.

Such an attitude, which is limited and embryonic in *The Wealth of Nations*, was bound to develop and become more explicit as techniques involving the use of connected stretches of the earth's surface and hence special rights of acquisition thereof, became a more prominent part of the apparatus of society. It cannot be said, however, to have developed as early as might have been expected, at any rate where the works of the nineteenth-century classical writers were concerned. Bentham in the *Constitutional Code* provides for an 'Interior Communication Minister' with *inter alia* 'Aqua-procurative or water supply-securing' and 'Malaria-obviating' functions; and it was under Benthamite influence that the vast developments of governmental activity in this latter respect took place. But on the majority of the members of the London Political Economy Club, absorbed in discussion of free trade, the currency and the measure of value, etc., the great development of public utility functions and the railways made comparatively little impact.[1] The systematic discussion of the economic problems of railways in Lardner's splendid *Railway Economy* came from one who stood right outside the tradition. His conclusion 'that bodies which possess the almost exclusive control of the intercourse of the country . . . have none of the qualities and ought to have none of the privileges attaching to private commercial establishment — that they have not been created . . . by the unaided efforts of individuals . . . that they owe their origin and existence to the will of the legislature expressed

[1] In the records of the Club, matters of this sort were only discussed on nine occasions in the first fifty years of its existence.

in the various acts of incorporation and . . . to the legislature they must be held in a peculiar degree responsible' finds no parallel in the writings of the majority of the classical economists.

Nevertheless, the attitude and the spirit of Adam Smith's recommendation regarding turnpikes emerges and becomes explicit with John Stuart Mill, who, despite the ambiguity of his hopes regarding small co-operative societies, must still be regarded as an exponent of the main position of the system of economic freedom. Both in his discussion of production on a large scale in the *Principles*[1] and in his little-known letter on the water supply of London,[2] Mill argues for the recognition of the direct public interest in such enterprises. So far as railways were concerned he declared himself against the alleged waste of capital and land involved in duplication and argued that only one such line should be permitted: 'but the control over that line ought not to be parted with by the state except on a temporary concession as in France'. As regards water supply, he declared that were there in being a municipal government for the whole of London, he would be in favour of making over to it a function so important as that of water supply.

In each of these cases Mill's reasoning is clear. The case of leaving supply to private agency rests on the possibility of competition. By this it is clear that neither he nor any other classical economist meant mathematically pure competition only; he would have been satisfied with something much more rough and ready than that; he would have been slightly impatient at some of the quite unrealistic refinements which have emerged in this connection. But both with railways and water supply there was no possibility of competition without, as he thought, the likelihood of a substantial waste of resources. Hence the business of supply

---

[1] Mill, *Principles of Political Economy*, vol. ii, pp. 141–2.

[2] Mill, *The Regulation of the London Water Supply* (1851), reprinted in *Essays on Economics and Society*, pp. 431–8. On the episode of Mill's intervention in the water supply controversy, Pedro Schwarz's interesting article 'John Stuart Mill and Laissez Faire: London Water', *Economica* (Feb. 1966) should be consulted.

became a matter for some sort of public control — either by way of ownership and management or regulated concession. In all this, Mill may have put a sharper edge on his argument than some. But I am sure that his attitude is typical of the general conception of the place of public utility enterprise in the organisation of production which has prevailed since that day among economists of the liberal school. The so-called system of economic freedom is out of perspective if this important complement is left out.

8. WAKEFIELD AND COLONIES

These propositions with regard to public utility undertakings may be regarded as supplementary to the system of economic freedom rather than critical of its central contentions. We now have to take account of criticisms which questioned outright its applicability in certain contexts for providing a suitable organisation for development.

The first of these has been mentioned already in the discussion of the population problem. Where the development of unoccupied areas was concerned, Gibbon Wakefield argued that unlimited scope for free settlement was inimical to the achievement of an appropriate division of labour; and that, therefore, a price should be placed upon land so as to prevent undue dispersion. This was a central feature of his theory of colonisation. His argument persuaded Jeremy Bentham, who christened the resulting rule of action 'The vicinity maximization' or 'the dispersion-preventing principle';[1] and it was attempted to put the rule into operation in the South Australian experiment. In the discussion of the limits of the *laissez-faire* principle in John Stuart Mill's *Principles*, it is specifically cited as an exemplification of one of these limits. 'However beneficial it might be to the colony in the aggregate, and to each individual composing it, that no one should occupy

[1] See R. C. Mills, *The Colonization of Australia* (1915) pp. 152–3.

more land than he can properly cultivate, nor become a proprietor until there are other labourers ready to take his place in working for hire; it can never be the interest of an individual to exercise this forbearance, unless he is assured that others will do so too. . . . It is the interest of each to do what is good for all, but only if others will do likewise.'[1]

9. THE INFANT INDUSTRIES ARGUMENT

Wakefield's strictures, although capable of being conceived as being a special case of a much wider principle, in themselves related only to the very unusual situation of a new society in entirely unoccupied territory.   Much more important, both for practice and for its inroads into an important area of the system of economic freedom, was the celebrated argument for protection of infant industries.   This arises, of course, in connection with the affairs of societies having trade connections with other parts of the world, a situation we have not had to discuss so far.   But fundamentally, as we shall see, it raises issues transcending this circumstance; and although it is possible to argue, as I should argue, that these issues can be enormously exaggerated, yet their theoretical significance is very considerable.

Proposals for the protection of nascent industries are to be found very far back.   In his authoritative *Studies in the Theory of International Trade*, Professor Jacob Viner is able to cite a page of quotations from writers of the mercantilist period, in which protection is solicited for special industries on the ground that they are still in their infancy, and to refer to further examples of such arguments in Steuart and Tucker.[2]   But the real development of the argument as a critique of the working of a free system comes later.

---

[1] Mill, *op. cit.*, p. 959.
[2] Jacob Viner, *op. cit.* (1937) pp. 70–1.   The writers cited are Yarranton, Wood, Dobbs and Bindon, and the references are to Steuart's *Principles of Political Economy* (1767) and Tucker's *Instructions to Travellers* (1757) p. 33.

Adam Smith was not impressed by the case presented by these early writers. He was willing to concede that on occasion 'By means of such regulations [high duties, etc.] . . . a particular manufacture may sometimes be acquired sooner than it could have been otherwise, and after a certain time may be made at home as cheap or cheaper than in the foreign country'. But he thought that it did not follow: 'that the sum total either of . . . industry, or revenue, can ever be augmented by any such regulation. The industry of the society can augment only in proportion as its capital augments, and its capital can augment only in proportion to what can be saved out of . . . revenue. But the immediate effect of every such regulation is to diminish . . . revenue, and what diminishes . . . revenue is certainly not very likely to augment . . . capital faster than it would have augmented of its own accord, had both capital and industry been left to find out their natural requirements.'[1]

It was this position which provoked systematic opposition and the exposition of a different point of view. In this movement the originating influence, and perhaps the most important from the practical point of view, was the argument developed in Alexander Hamilton's celebrated *Report on Manufactures*. This is a very temperate yet powerful statement, written in 1791, of the case for encouraging the growth of manufacturing industry in the United States. Part of this case rests upon apprehension of unfair competition by established industries abroad and, although practically important, has no fundamental bearing on the theory of development as such. But part of it rests upon the alleged necessity of government encouragement to offset the inertia of habit and the 'fear of want of success in untried enterprises'; and this of course goes to the root of the matter. As a practical down-to-earth plea for government intervention in such connections, Hamilton's advocacy could hardly be bettered.

But if we are looking for pure excellence of intellectual analysis, the palm must clearly go to John Rae. Rae's chapter, in the *New Principles of Political Economy*, on the 'Identity of National

[1] Smith, *op. cit.*, vol. i, pp. 422–3.

Individual Interests considered as a theoretical Principle' may
not have had wide practical influence, but it is certainly by far the
most distinguished exposition of the case for the public support of
infant industry in the whole range of the relevant literature. Rae
has all the usual arguments in favour of support for the special
risks of starting new enterprise in the face of established competition. But he digs much deeper than this. He tackles Adam
Smith on his fundamental assumptions in this respect. Is it true,
as Smith had contended, that an earlier gain of skill makes no
difference to potential revenue and saving? No, he argues,
'Individuals as well as nations acquire wealth from other sources
than mere saving from revenue . . . skill is as necessary, and consequently as valuable a co-operator with the industry of both as
either capital or parsimony.'[1] And if this is true of individuals,
how much truer is it of nations where the acquisition of skill is
less transitory than that of a single lifetime. Adam Smith, in
his historical discussion of the progress of opulence, himself
shows that the arrival of manufacturers in agrarian communities
has been a great benefit. To maintain that positive encouragement
of such arrival is never advisable he must show that such developments will always take place without it, and that he would find it
hard to do. Nevertheless, Rae argues, the legislator must be
cautious: 'He is never justified in attempting to transfer arts . . .
from foreign countries to his own, unless he have sufficient reason
to conclude that they will ultimately lessen the cost of the commodities they produce, or are of such a nature, that the risk of
waste to the stock of the community from a sudden interruption
to their importation from abroad, is sufficiently great to warrant
the probable expense both of the transfer and of maintaining the
manufacture at home.'[2]

It was this sort of argument — it may even have been Rae's
arguments — that led John Stuart Mill, in the course of his
animadversions on the errors involved in current arguments
for protection, to make his famous exception in regard to the protection of infant industries. 'The superiority of one country over

[1] Rae, *op. cit.*, p. 61.   [2] Ibid., p. 367.

another in a branch of production often arises only from having begun it sooner.... A country which has ... skill and experience yet to acquire may in other respects be better adapted to the production than those which were earlier in the field. . . . But it cannot be expected that individuals should, at their own risk, or rather to their certain loss, introduce a new manufacture, and bear the burden of carrying it until the producers have been educated up to the level of those with whom the processes are traditional. A protecting duty, continued for a reasonable time, might sometimes be the least inconvenient mode in which the nation can tax itself for the support of such an experiment.'[1]

Poor Mill; such an admission from such an authority was made the pretext for all sorts of practices which he regarded as quite indefensible. In 1868, writing to an Australian correspondent, he complains that the abuses have been such as greatly to shake the opinion expressed in the *Principles* and 'though I still think that the introduction of the foreign industry is worth a sacrifice, and that a temporary protecting duty, if it were sure to remain temporary, would probably be the best shape in which that sacrifice can be made, I am inclined to believe that it is safer to make it by an annual grant from the public treasury, which is not nearly so likely to be continued indefinitely, to prop up an industry which has not so thriven as to be able to dispense with it'.[2] With this sort of qualification, the infant industry argument passes into the generally accepted corpus of classical and neo-classical tradition. It is taken more or less for granted both by Sidgwick and by Marshall.

10. EXTERNAL ECONOMIES

Up to this point I have explained the argument for this kind of intervention in terms of the advantages accruing from the development of particular processes or industries. It should be reasonably obvious, however, that it is capable of being carried

[1] John Stuart Mill, *Principles of Political Economy*, p. 918–19.
[2] John Stuart Mill, *Letters*, ed. Hugh Elliot (1910) vol. ii, p. 149.

substantially further than this. The fostering of certain types of economic activity in this way may be conceived to give rise to what Marshall called external economies in the shape of a more generally skilled and adaptable labour force, the prevalence in the locality or society concerned of general traditions of industrial know-how, the existence of organs of technical information and research, a trade press and so on. It is customary to think of the Marshallian external economies in the context of the expansion of particular industries. But, in fact, the conception is much more at home in a wider setting; and it is no accident that it was first elaborated by Marshall in his *Principles*, not in book v which deals with demand and supply and value, but in book IV which deals with land, labour, capital and organisation.

It was this kind of influence which, much earlier than Marshall, had been the focus of List's various disquisitions on the development of productive powers. List was a turbulent, tragic character, full of romantic prejudices and given to wild exaggeration, and his misrepresentation of his intellectual antagonists, particularly Adam Smith, is almost comic in its inaccuracy.[1] But, divested of its sound and fury, there remains surely a core of truth in his contention that the fostering of certain industries in certain historic context may carry with it an increase of productive potential, not to be measured merely in the value of particular outputs or the growth of capital values. In my judgment the influence of his exaggerations and misrepresentations did much harm, especially in so far as they contributed to the growth of economic nationalism in Europe. But that is no reason for denying some degree of analytical validity to his principal contention.

It is worth noting that all the writers I have cited developed the argument for the encouragement of infant industries in the context of national societies open to competition from elsewhere. They did not contend that pure economic freedom was inappropriate within closed societies or between different localities within the national area. List, indeed, who was busy agitating for the forma-

[1] On this see Nicholson's introduction to Lloyd's translation of List, *The National System of Political Economy* (1904).

tion of the great free trade area which was the Zollverein, went out of his way to declare that within a universal confederation 'there would be no better way of raising all these countries [the membership of the confederation] to the same stage of wealth and cultivation as England than free trade'.[1] Nevertheless, the formal arguments developed had wider implications than that even though, from a practical point of view, List's reservations may not be thought to be thoroughly sensible. It is not without significance that the first mention by Marshall in his *Principles* of the concept of external economies occurs in conjunction with the phrase, the localisation of industry.[2] At any rate it is clear to me that the very cautious and open-ended expositions by Sidgwick and Marshall of the claims of the system of economic freedom were substantially influenced by the inroads on the more dogmatic versions which had been made by the infant industry argument. The presumption is still in favour of economic freedom as the central principle. But there is a wide margin left for various types of intervention.

II. THE INSTABILITY OF AGGREGATE DEMAND

There is a further respect in which the progress of analysis has tended to modify thought in regard to the System of Natural Liberty.

Adam Smith's picture of the self-regulating mechanism of the market related essentially to the allocation of resources in a system in which the utilisation of capacity was reasonably full. By which I am sure that neither he nor any sensible writer on these subjects would have understood a state of affairs in which at any moment there were no persons moving from job to job and no machines or sites in process of adaptation or transformation, and consequently,

[1] List, *National System of Political Economy*, trs. Lloyd (1904) pp. 105–6.
[2] Marshall, *Principles of Economics*, 8th ed. (1920) p. 266.

E

if registers were kept, zero unemployment or one hundred per cent use of capacity. That could only have been plausible on the assumption of the stationary state from which most of them hoped that we were far distant. But they certainly thought that disturbances of a fairly full use of capacity were abnormal and transitory. Those who believed in Say's Law, or its equivalent, thought that a state of general under-utilisation was impossible, all disturbances being particular. Even those who believed that disturbances of general equilibrium were conceivable were apt to treat them as if they were bound to be transitory and subject to a self-regulating mechanism of their own.

Since the middle of the nineteenth century, however, this assumption has tended to weaken. The systematic statistical study of the trade cycle, from Jevons and Juglar onwards, revealed recurrent periods when under-utilisation has prevailed; and the analysis of theoretical models of the economy in general and the capital market in particular has shown various ways in which such situations may occur.

Hence the assumptions that the utilisation of resources as a whole was a process which could be left to look after itself has also been weakened. The door has been opened to speculation regarding the possibility of controls and policies tending to reduce oscillations and to secure a more even utilisation of resources; and in so far as it can be argued — which has been questioned by some authorities from Robertson downwards — that growth is best fostered in the absence of such fluctuations, the theory of development has also been affected.

Most of this speculation has taken place so recently as to fall outside the main focus of this survey. But some of it takes its rise in the theories of accumulation which we have already examined and some in the theories of money to which I am about to proceed. In the context of the present lecture, all that is necessary to note in this connection is that, in so far as it has been thought possible to devise mechanisms for ensuring smoother evolution of the free enterprise mechanism, to that extent a further case has been established for functions of government additional to those originally contemplated in the view of the free enterprise system first elaborated in the eighteenth century.

NOTE

COLLECTIVISM AND GROWTH

It would be interesting to conclude this survey with some account of the theories of collectivist development. But alas, such theories are difficult to find. Nineteenth-century socialism furnishes little or no overt discussion of this problem. Utopian socialism was essentially a project of distributive justice, its assumptions as regards production were nebulous in the extreme. And although Marx and Engels had much to say of the catastrophic tendencies of capitalism, they discouraged discussion of the organisation of the society which was to replace it. In more recent times there have been numerous attempts to demonstrate the possibility of price systems under collectivism, of which the constructions of Barone, Lange and Lerner are the most notable and thought-provoking. But the plausibility of these constructions derives very largely from statical assumptions: it is not easy to see how they work under changing conditions. Speaking broadly, I should say that the most impressive claim that can be made for collectivism in regard to development relates to the possibilities of capital accumulation. Under authoritarian collectivism, it is arguable that the pace of accumulation can be made to be greater than it would be under looser conditions — you are said to arrive at Ramsey's Bliss somewhat sooner. But on the whole, even at the present day, though the literature of particular plans is extensive, it would be difficult to point to any very coherent body of work relating to the theory of collectivist growth as such. It may be that development of the *how* theories to which I alluded in my first lecture will fill this gap. But in the meantime it must be admitted, as a Soviet official once admitted to Hugh Dalton, that this is a subject where until now practice has preceded theory — or at any rate systematic theory.

THE PLACE OF MONEY IN THE THEORY OF DEVELOPMENT

1. INTRODUCTORY

I have now passed in review the main features of the history of thought in regard to what the classical economists would have called productive factors and their organisation in the process of economic development. But so far I have said nothing, save incidentally, about money and credit and their functions in this respect. This clearly is an omission which must be remedied. The part played by money and its vicissitudes in promoting or retarding economic development has probably occupied more space in the relevant literature than any other single subject, indeed perhaps more than all the other single subjects put together. Needless to say, I shall not attempt to cover this material in all its bewildering variety. My aim is only to exhibit the main issues in the broadest historical perspective. I shall deal first with thought concerning the qualitative functions of money and monetary institutions in regard to development, and then with discussions of the effect of variations in its quantity.

2. MONEY AS A PREREQUISITE OF DEVELOPMENT

To begin with the existence of money as an essential prerequisite of development. Perception of the inconvenience of barter begins very early indeed. It is to be discerned in the discussions of money-making in Aristotle's *Politics*.[1] The probable lack of

[1] Aristotle, *Politics*, trs. Welldon, 2nd ed. (1888) p. 23.

coincidence of wants in the absence of a medium of exchange is explicitly stated by the Roman jurist, Paulus; and whether because of this or by reason of independent reflection the same point was emphasised by St Thomas Aquinas and thereafter by other scholastic writers and mercantilist pamphleteers.[1] So that by the time, 1705, that John Law came to write his famous tract *Money and Trade Considered* — in spite of its fateful recommendations for policy, the repository of so many brilliant intuitions regarding finance — the theory of the subject had become self-conscious and explicit.

Law's formulation was succinct and authoritative. The 'state of barter was inconvenient and disadvantageous:

' 1. He who desired to barter would not always find people who wanted the goods he had, and had such goods as he desired in exchange.

2. Contracts taken payable in goods were uncertain for goods of the same kind differed in value.

3. There was no measure by which the proportion of value goods had to one another could be known.

In this state of barter there was little trade and few artsmen. . . . The losses and difficulties . . . would force the landed-men to a greater consumption of the goods of their own product, and a lesser consumption of other goods.' [2]

It was in some such form as this, or something less well developed, that the theory of the subject was transmitted through the works of the classical period from Adam Smith to John Stuart Mill.[3] It was not until Walras that the matter was further refined by his beautiful demonstration that, even where there existed a qualita-

---

[1] On the evolution of thought in this connection, see A. E. Monroe: *Monetary Theory before Adam Smith* (Cambridge, Mass., 1923) especially parts i and ii.

[2] John Law, *Money and Trade Considered* (1750) pp. 6–7.

[3] Smith, *The Wealth of Nations*, pp. 22–6 ; Mill, *Principles of Political Economy*, p. 502. The *locus classicus* of all this is usually supposed to be Joseph Harris, *An Essay upon Money and Coins* (1757–8) pp. 34–5. But Law's is clearly the superior statement.

tive coincidence of wants, in the absence of a medium of indirect exchange, it would be a matter of pure accident if the ratios of exchange between pairs of commodities were mutually consistent.[1]

There is one exception to this sequence from Aristotle onwards of variations on a hackneyed theme.   In his *Della Moneta*, Galiani demonstrates, in a context of much broader considerations, the necessity of money for any advanced community in a way which deserves much more notice than it has hitherto received in the literature of the subject.[2]   He takes the inconveniences of barter more or less for granted and asks why these cannot be avoided by a communistic organisation such as actually exists in the establishment of religious orders.   The difficulty, he contends, arises because in larger communities it is not possible to count on the same sense of obligation and honesty as prevails in small élites where everyone may be counted on to do his fair share of work and to contribute the full fruits of his labour to the common pool.   But this, he suggests, could be circumnavigated by the issue of tickets acknowledging the receipt of goods and thus entitling the producer to others.   These tickets obviously should be eligible for the procurement of more than one other type of commodity and for this purpose, it would be necessary that equivalences should be established: a bushel of corn being equal to so much wine, meat, oil, clothing, cheese, etc.   This system would be liable to fraud if the tickets were issued by the various entrepôts.   But this could be remedied if they were all issued by the Prince. . . .   At this point Galiani recognises that what he has done is to recreate the actual conditions of the world, whereby through the use of money and prices it is possible to transcend the miserable condition in which each works only for himself and achieve a state of affairs in which each is working for society in general; and this, not by relying on virtue or piety, motives not present in sufficient

[1] Léon Walras, *Éléments d'Économie Pure* (1926) pp. 115–21.   See also Wicksell, *Lectures on Political Economy* (1934–5) vol. i, pp. 63–8, where this important theorem is expanded with considerably greater expository economy.

[2] Galiani, *Della Moneta Libri Cinque* (Napoli, 1750) pp. 89–95.

abundance in large societies, but on the force of individual interest and its urge to satisfaction. . . . My summary, which perforce omits many felicitous details, including the introduction of a tax system, can give only a faint impression of the elegance and force of Galiani's argument. As M. Bousquet has rightly remarked, it is 'une grande page de la littérature économique mondiale'.[1]

Even Galiani, however, is very general. He shows together with the rest that the existence of money is essential if economic life is to have any degree of complexity. But his demonstration, equally with that of all the others who have expatiated on the inconveniences of barter, is not explicitly focused on the connection between the use of money and the development of the economic system. For such focus we have to go to Turgot who in his *Réflexions sur la Formation et la Distribution des Richesses* puts money right in the centre of this picture.

'The more money came to stand for everything else', he says, 'the more possible did it become for each person, by devoting himself entirely to the kind of cultivation or industry he had chosen, to relieve himself of all care for the satisfaction of his other wants, and to think only how he could obtain as much money as possible by the sale of his fruits or his labour, very sure that by means of this money he can get all the rest. It is thus that the employment of money has prodigiously hastened the progress of society.'[2] This puts money into direct relation with the progress consequent on the division of labour. Later on it is linked with increased facility for the accumulation of capital: 'the ease with which it (money) can be accumulated has made it the most sought-after of moveable riches and has furnished the means to augment (their) quantity unceasingly simply by means of economy'.[3] All of which is

[1] In his introduction to the French translation of this work, *De la monnaie* (Paris, 1955) p. 21.

[2] *Op. cit.* para. xlviii. I have used the translation of the Harvard Economic Classics, p. 42. The original passage is to be found in Daire's edition of the *Œuvres de Turgot* (1844) vol. i, p. 32.

[3] Ibid., para. lviii, p. 50. I have substituted 'their' for 'its' in this translation, the sense of the original (Daire, vol. i, p. 36) clearly referring to 'richesses mobiliaires' rather than to money.

obvious enough. But I do not know any other place in the literature where it is put with comparable simplicity and force.

3. CREDIT AS A SUBSTITUTE FOR CASH

The theory of the significance for economic growth of the existence of money, although universally applicable, was developed at times when coins made from the precious metals were the principal media of exchange. As economic life became more complex, as the use of metallic money became supplemented by the use of financial instruments of one kind or another, there developed theories of the functions of credit which must also be noticed in this context. For the purposes of this narrative we may regard these theories as covering both convertible notes — inconvertible paper counting as money proper — and bank credit in other forms. In fact of course there was much controversy about the similarities and dissimilarities of such instruments; but this was scarcely relevant to the discussion of the significance of credit for economic development.

In this connection we may begin with some notice of the opinions of David Hume. Law touches on the convenience of paper instruments in his famous tract; but the burden of his propaganda for credit based on land was the alleged desirability of increasing the supply of money, a matter to be dealt with later. It is Hume whose reflections may be regarded as seminal in respect of the question now under discussion.

Hume's approach to this question arises in the famous essay *Of the Balance of Trade*. In the course of a discussion of the equilibrating mechanism in international payments he demonstrates that between economies in which the sole means of circulation are currencies of similar metallic composition, the effect of specie flows on prices and incomes must be to produce tendencies to correct any lack of balance in reciprocal payments; and he argues that, in such circumstances, the forces governing payments between *countries* are essentially similar to the forces governing payments between *counties*. 'Did not long experience make people easy on this head, what a fund of gloomy reflections might calculations afford to a melancholy *Yorkshireman* while he computed and magnified the sums drawn to *London* by taxes, absentees, commodities and found on comparison the opposite articles so much inferior.'[1]   But then he sees the possibility of disturbing circumstances — 'one expedient by which it is possible to sink . . . money below its natural level in any kingdom', namely credit instruments additional to the equilibrium amounts of specie. 'I scarcely know any method of sinking money below its level, but those institutions of banks, funds and paper-credit which are so much practised in this kingdom. These render paper equivalent to money, circulate it throughout the whole state, make it supply the place of gold and silver, raise proportionally the price of labour and commodities, and by that means either banish a great part of these precious metals, or prevent their further increase.'[2]

The judgement thus far is adverse. But then, in a late edition of the essay, with that wonderful capacity for seeing all round a question which makes Hume perhaps the most thought-provoking of all writers on our subject, he changes key: 'It must', he says, 'however be confessed that, as all these questions of trade and money are extremely complicated, there are certain lights in which this subject may be placed so as to represent the advantages of paper credit and banks to be superior to their disadvantages. That they banish specie and bullion from a state is undoubtedly true; and whoever looks no further than this circumstance does well to condemn them; but specie and bullion are not of so great consequence as not to admit of a compensation, and even an overbalance

---

[1] David Hume, *Writings on Economics*, ed. Rotwein (Edinburgh, 1955) pp. 70. All further references to Hume's economic essays are to this edition.

[2] Ibid., pp. 67–8. There is a very clear anticipation of this point of view in the remarkable tract by Isaac Gervaise, *The System or Theory of the Trade of the World*, discovered by Professor Viner and edited by Professor J. M. Letiche in the Johns Hopkins Series, *A Reprint of Economic Tracts* (Baltimore, 1954).

E 2

from the increase of industry and credit which may be promoted by the right use of paper money.' He then goes on to depict, in a masterly manner, the way in which business operations are facilitated by a system in which it is not necessary to maintain reserves of ready money in order to finance irregular transactions. 'It is well known of what advantage it is to a merchant to be able to discount his bills on occasion: and everything that facilitates this species of traffic is favourable to the general commerce of a state.'[1]

In these few remarks, which as we have seen were essentially in the nature of a digression and an afterthought, we can see anticipation of analyses of the advantages of banking which subsequently became standard theory — the advantages of economising metal and of elasticity of means of payment.

The theory of the advantage of economy of metal receives its classic statement in *The Wealth of Nations*. Adam Smith accepted the conclusion, springing from Hume's analysis, that at any given time in any open economy there was an appropriate volume of means of payment; and that if, because of the institution of banks and such-like institutions, this amount was exceeded, the result would be the disappearance of gold and silver to the extent of the excess. But whereas for Hume this was recognition of a possible disadvantage, for Adam Smith it was exactly the contrary. The maintenance of a metallic currency involved an expense far greater than the maintenance of an equivalent amount of paper. If, therefore, paper credit could be substituted for metal without endangering the ultimate convertibility of whatever notes or other instruments came to be presented, there would be a definite saving of expense and a potential gain of directly productive capital. Gold and silver money were, so to speak, dead stock. 'The judicious operations of banking', he argued, 'by substituting paper in the room of a great part of this gold and silver, enables the country to convert a great part of this dead stock into active and productive stock. . . . The gold and silver money which circulates in any country may very properly be compared to a highway, which, while it circulates and carries to market all the

[1] Ibid., p. 70.

grass and corn of the country, produces itself not a single pile of either. The judicious operations of banking, by providing, if I may be allowed so violent a metaphor, a sort of waggon-way through the air, enable the country to convert, as it were, a great part of its highways into good pastures and cornfields, and thereby to increase very considerably the annual produce of its land and labour.'[1]

From this time onward, the function of credit instruments in economising the use of the precious metals as money was generally acknowledged. It receives its classic recognition in Ricardo's *Proposals for An Economical and Secure Currency* under which the whole internal legal tender circulation was to be notes convertible on demand not into coin but into bullion, thus effectively restricting the use of gold and silver to international transactions. For this it was explicitly claimed by its author that its greatest advantage would be the provision of 'the very cheap medium, paper, instead of the very valuable medium, gold; thereby enabling the country to derive all the profit which may be obtained by the productial employment of a capital to that amount'.[2] And in introducing this scheme, he had written that 'the introduction of the precious metals for the purposes of money may with truth be considered as one of the most important steps towards the improvement of commerce, and the arts of civilized life; but it is no less true that with the advancement of knowledge and science, we discover that it would be another improvement to banish them again from the employment in which, during a less enlightened period, they had been so advantageously applied'.[3] We need go no further forward than Ricardo to record this conception of the function of credit instruments as fully established.

The advantages — or alleged advantages — of the elasticity of paper credit are chiefly discussed in the historic literature in relation to the advantages — or alleged advantages — of increases in means of payment in general; and there will be much to be said of this discussion later on. But from time to time there

[1] Smith, *op. cit.*, vol. i, p. 304.
[2] Ricardo, *Works*, vol. iv, p. 70.   [3] Ibid., p. 65.

emerge arguments for the advantages of elasticity which do not involve the assumption of continuous increase; and although, in the nature of things, these do not loom large in the broad perspective of the possible influences on growth, they deserve some mention, if only in order to clear the way for discussion of the wider question.

The central point in this connection was put very vividly at an early stage by Cantillon: 'Though I consider a general Bank is in reality of very little solid service in a great State', he said, 'I allow that there are circumstances in which a Bank may have effects which seem astonishing. In a city where there are public debts for considerable amounts, the facility of a Bank enables one to buy and sell capital stock for enormous sums without causing any disturbance in the circulation.'[1]

But perhaps the most sophisticated statement of the advantages of this kind of elasticity was made, curiously enough, by Ricardo, who, as we shall see, in other respects was distinctly sceptical of any beneficial effects of deviations of the quantity of money from what it would be, were the circulation purely metallic: 'a currency is in its most perfect state', he had written, 'when it consists wholly of paper money, but of paper money of an equal value with the gold which it professes to represent'.[2] Nevertheless, in his *Proposals for an Economical and Secure Currency* he argues the merits of a paper circulation, not only on the ground that it economises the use of the precious metals and thus releases capital for productive investment, but also because it can meet upward fluctuations in the demand for liquidity without delay and without involving eventual changes in the value of money. The paragraph in which this argument is presented is perhaps worth quoting in full: 'Whenever merchants . . . have a want of confidence in each other, which disinclines them to deal on credit, or to accept in payment each other's checks, notes or bills; more money, whether it be paper or metallic money, is in demand; and the advantage of a paper circulation, when established on correct

[1] Cantillon, *Essai sur la Nature du Commerce*, p. 315.
[2] Ricardo, *Works*, vol. i, p. 361.

principles, is, that this additional quantity can be presently supplied without occasioning any variation in the value of the whole currency, either as compared with bullion or with any other commodity; whereas with a system of metallic currency, this additional quantity cannot be so readily supplied, and when it is finally supplied, the whole of the currency, as well as bullion, has acquired an increased value.'[1]

It would be possible to give further examples.[2] In the main, however, as I have already said, discussion of the advantages for development of the existence of credit instruments is usually associated with discussion of the advantages of increases in the volume of purchasing power in general. To the history of such discussion, therefore, we must now proceed.

4. MERCANTILISM AND THE SUPPLY OF MONEY

In approaching this subject, it is useful to realise that it is concerned almost exclusively with the virtue — or absence of virtue — of *increases* in the volume of money. No question in the whole range of economic controversy has been more extensively discussed both in time or in space. But, so far as I know, there has been no advocacy in the interests of growth, of *reductions*. From time to time when, by reason of clipping or the suspension of convertibility, currencies have become depreciated, there has been advocacy of restoration of the old standard, which carried with it some deflation. But this has been in the alleged interests of the maintenance of confidence or justice to creditors rather than in the direct interests of development, although doubtless many of the proponents of such policies would argue that in the long run development

[1] Ricardo, *Works*, vol. iv, p. 58. It is perhaps worth noting that in the same tract Ricardo puts forward a plan for diminishing the pressure on the money market due to large quarterly payments to public creditors, by authorising the issue of dividend warrants 'a few days *before* [*sic*] the receivers general are required to pay their balances into the Exchequer'—another case of provision for credit elasticity. Ibid., pp. 74–6.

[2] See, e.g. Mill, *Principles of Political Economy*, pp. 515–16.

would be helped rather than hindered by long-run continuity of historic values. Again, when the speculative activities of a boom have collapsed, there have sometimes been voices arguing that the temporary recession of spending is conducive to efficiency in that it eliminates bad investments and is a spur to innovation and reconstruction. But I know no instance where it has been suggested that continuing reductions in the volume of money would have a directly beneficial effect on development. In so far as it is suggested that variations are beneficial, the argument always relates to increases.

It is in this sense that we must interpret the main position of mercantilism. The different grounds which may be discovered for the persistent emphasis of the exponents of what Adam Smith called the mercantile theory of wealth on the desirability of a favourable balance of payments are many and various. As Professor Viner has shown, they used so many arguments to justify their position that any short statement thereof is liable to be misleading.[1] But I do not think we go seriously wrong if we assume that underlying a great deal, though not all, of their detailed arguments was a conviction that an increase in the volume of money was somehow or other good for trade and generally beneficial to economic activity.

This point of view is very clearly expressed in Rice Vaughan's *Discourse of Coin and Coinage* (1675) where it is stated that policies directed to 'the increase of money and the Materials thereof' carry with them the benefit of 'The increase of Trade and Manufacture which are always best managed, where money doth most abound' and further that 'The abundance likewise of Money doth enable Tenants the better to pay their Rents, and all men in general to keep up and maintain their credits and to pay all public Charges and Contributions.'[2]

---

[1] See the masterly chapters (I and II) in Viner, *Studies in the Theory of International Trade* (1937).

[2] *Op. cit.*, reprinted by McCulloch in his *Select Collection of Scarce and Valuable Tracts on Money* (Political Economy Club, 1856) pp. 74-5.

There are many expressions of such sentiments scattered about the literature of this period. They receive, however, what is perhaps their most sophisticated expression in the tract by John Law from which I have already quoted. As is well known, Law was seeking support for a banking project which would have based the issue of money on the value of land rather than gold and silver; he explicitly recommended this proposal on the ground that it would permit an increase in the volume of money and that without such an increase affairs in Scotland would languish. 'Considering how small a share we have of the money of Europe', he urged, 'and how much trade depends upon money: it will not be found very practicable to better our condition, but by an addition to our money or if it is practicable without it, it is much more so with it.'[1] And he goes on to argue, as some writers of our own period of full employment have argued, that an increase need not be accompanied by a serious fall in the value of money since 'all sorts of manufacture would be cheaper, because in greater quantity: and all goods imported would be cheaper, money being easier borrowed, merchants would deal for a greater value, and men of estates would be capacitate [*sic*] to trade and able to sell at less profit.'[2] Only reference to diminishing returns to scale and the spreading of overheads is lacking completely to anticipate the position of some modern economists in this connection!

5. THE ANTI-MERCANTILIST REACTION

Such attitudes provoked a reaction. Law's plans, when translated into action in France, ended in one of the most damaging inflationary booms and collapses in history; and Cantillon, who, after being threatened with expulsion by Law, had made a fortune out

---

[1] Law, *Money and Trade Considered* (1750) p. 107. The eccentric punctuation follows the original.
[2] Ibid., p. 142.

of his prescience of disaster, scarcely veiled his contempt for the outlook from which it sprang. In the *Essai sur la Nature du Commerce*, written before 1734 — the year of the author's death — the emphasis is all upon what we should call the 'real' determinants of economic activity — the role of Land as 'the Source or Matter from whence all Wealth is produced' and Labour 'the form which produces it'.[1] It contains one of the best and most intimately informed discussions of money and the exchanges ever written, but it goes out of its way to deny any great advantage from abundance of money. 'An abundance of fictitious and imaginary money', he wrote, 'causes the same disadvantages as an increase of real money in circulation, by raising the price of Land and Labour, or by making works and manufactures more expensive at the risk of subsequent loss. But this furtive abundance vanishes at the first gust of discredit and precipitates disorder.'[2]

But Cantillon's *Essai* was not published until 1755: and although there were clearly versions both in English and in French circulating before that date, it is doubtful whether it had any significant influence on thought in this respect. The decisive *coup de grâce* to the view that the abundance of money as such — as distinct from its increase — is unimportant was given by David Hume in his essay *On Money* in his *Political Discourses* which were published in 1752: 'Money', he wrote, 'is none of the wheels of trade; it is the oil which renders the motion of the wheels more smooth and easy. If we consider any one kingdom by itself, it is evident, that the greater or less plenty of money is of no consequence; since the prices of commodities are always proportioned to the plenty of money, and a crown in Harry VII's time served the same purpose as a pound does at present',[3] and again, 'Where coin is in greater plenty; as a greater quantity of it is required to

---

[1] Cantillon, *Essai sur la Nature du Commerce*, p. 3.

[2] Ibid., p. 311. For a significant comparison of the ideas of Law and Cantillon in this respect, Charles Rist, *Histoire des Doctrines relatives au Crédit et à la Monnaie depuis John Law jusqu'à nos Jours* (Paris, 1938) pp. 20–57 should be consulted.

[3] Hume, *Writings on Economics*, p. 33.

represent the same quantity of goods; it can have no effect either good or bad, taking a nation within itself; any more than it would make an alteration on a merchant's books, if, instead of the ARABIAN method of notation which requires few characters, he should make use of the ROMAN, which requires a great many. Nay, the greater quantity of money, like the Roman characters, is rather inconvenient, and requires greater trouble to keep and transport it.'[1]

This approach to the question, although as we shall see not at all exhausting Hume's own contribution, had enormous influence. It was adopted in its entirety by Harris in his *Essay upon Money and Coins* without any qualification or mention of Hume's further discussion of the subject — the caption of the relevant section is 'A nation having no foreign commerce will not stand in need of any specific quantity of money.'[2] And it is fair to say that thenceforward insistence on the unimportance of money became standard practice in the classical tradition. Thus, for instance, J. S. Mill summarises his analysis of the functions of money in the *Principles* by insisting that 'There cannot, in short, be intrinsically a more insignificant thing, in the economy of society, than money; except in the character of a contrivance for sparing time and labour. It is a machine for doing quickly and commodiously, what would be done, though less quickly and commodiously, without it: and like many other kinds of machinery, it only exerts a distinct and independent influence of its own when it gets out of order.'[3] And later on, while actually recognising that the effect of an increase in the quantity of money depends in part on how and where it is introduced, he actually insists that 'these effects, however, would evidently proceed not from the mere increase of money, but *from accessory circumstances attending it*' (my italics).[4] Yet on the

---

[1] Ibid., p. 37.
[2] Harris, *An Essay upon Money and Coins* (1757–8) p. 80, also reprinted in *A Select Collection of Scarce and Valuable Tracts on Money* (Political Economy Club, 1856).
[3] Mill, *op. cit.*, p. 506.
[4] Ibid., p. 511.

basis of his accompanying analysis, which is a corrected version of Hume's discussion of the effects of an increase overnight of the money in every pocket, it is clear that some other effects are likely to accompany every increase in the quantity of money save in the limiting case when every cash and credit holding is increased exactly proportionately.

Mill's attitude in this respect is very typical. Although, as will emerge later, in fact he knew a good deal about the dynamic possibilities of changes in the quantity of money, yet in arranging the tone and proportion of his exposition, he preferred to soft-pedal these and to put all the emphasis on the unimportance from the statical point of view of the absolute quantity of money. Doubtless there were reasons for this. The inflationary events of the period of the suspension of cash payments had left an indelible impression on the minds of the classical economists from whom Mill learned his economics; and the period of his major intellectual inventiveness was also the period of the inflationary propaganda of the Birmingham School — the Gemini letters and so forth. But it involved a distortion of perspective; and eventually, in our own day, the persistence of such habits in some quarters provoked an equally one-sided reaction in which, so to speak, the *other* baby was now emptied out with the bath water, so that the monetary factor completely dominated the analysis of prosperity and the very real dangers of continuing inflation were treated as negligible.

This tradition is all the more remarkable in that the original treatment of the subject by Hume completely avoided its errors. Having shown that from a *static* point of view the quantity of money was unimportant, Hume went on to show that from a *dynamic* point of view *changes* in the quantity of money could have a very important influence. 'In every kingdom', he argues, 'into which money begins to flow in greater abundance than formerly, everything takes a new face: labour and industry gain life: the merchant becomes more enterprising, the manufacturer more diligent and skilful and even the farmer follows his plough with greater alacrity and attention', and he accounts for this in terms of a time lag between the increase of the quantity of money and its full impact on prices — in terms of the 'interval between the acquisition of money and rise of prices'.

The analysis is very explicit and is worth quoting at some length: 'When any quantity of money is imported into a nation, it is not at first dispersed into many hands, but is confined to the coffers of a few persons, who immediately seek to employ it to advantage. Here are a set of manufacturers or merchants, we shall suppose, who have received returns of gold and silver for goods which they sent to CADIZ. They are thereby enabled to employ more workmen than formerly, who never dream of demanding higher wages, but are glad of employment from such good paymasters. If workmen become scarce, the manufacturer gives higher wages, but at first requires an encrease of labour; and this is willingly submitted to by the artisan, who can now eat and drink better, to compensate his additional toil and fatigue. He carries his money to market where he finds every thing at the same price as formerly, but returns with greater quantity and of better kinds, for the use of his family. The farmer and gardener, finding, that all their commodities are taken off, apply themselves with alacrity to raising more; and at the same time can afford to take better and more cloths from their tradesmen, whose price is the same as formerly, and their industry only whetted by so much new gain. It is easy to trace the money in its progress through the whole commonwealth; where we shall find, that it must first quicken the diligence of every individual, before it encrease the price of labour.'

Hence it follows, he concludes, 'that it is of no manner of consequence, with regard to the domestic happeness of a state, whether money be in a greater or less quantity. The good policy of the magistrate consists only in keeping it, if possible, still encreasing.' And he goes on to depict the miserable state of a nation whose gold and silver decrease. The interval before adjustment is now 'as pernicious to industry . . . as it is advantageous when these metals are encreasing. The workman has not the same employment from the manufacturers and merchant; though he pays the same price for everything in the market. The farmer cannot dispose of his corn and cattle: though he must pay the same rent to his landlord. The poverty and beggary and sloth, which must ensue, are easily foreseen.'[1]

Can it have been the expression of such sentiments which occasioned Adam Smith's reference to his friend's ideas in his lectures: 'Mr. Hume's reasoning is exceedingly ingenious. He seems, however, to have gone a little into the notion that public opulence consists in money.'[2] Whatever the reason we may surely agree that neglect of such well-balanced analysis and insistence only on the static aspects thereof, was a grave blemish on much classical exposition.

6. MONEY AND EMPLOYMENT

Nevertheless it would be a mistake to assume that there was no analysis of the desirability of some increase in the quantity of money in a growing economy save in what Keynes called 'the underworlds of Karl Marx, Silvio Gesell or Major Douglas'.[3] On the contrary, when the classical economists were not thinking of the dreadful heresies of the Mercantile Theory of Wealth and the obvious undesirability of crude inflation, they said much which has considerable bearing on this very intricate matter, as the following survey will show.

It cannot be said that there was much discussion of the relation between monetary movements and employment. Law, clearly assuming a wage level rigid downwards and ignoring the distinction which Hume was to make between the significance of mere quantity and increases in quantity, had argued that 'Domestic

[1] Hume, *op. cit.*, pp. 37–40.
[2] Smith, *Lectures on Justice, Police, Revenue and Arms*, ed. Cannan (1896) p. 197.
[3] Keynes, *The General Theory of Employment, Interest, and Money* (1936) p. 32.

trade depends on the money. a greater quantity employs more people than a lesser quantity. a limited sum can only set a number of people to work proportioned to it, and 'tis with little success laws are made, for employing the poor or idle in countries where money is scarce.'[1] Hume, as we have seen, describes the beneficial effects on employment when money increases; and much later, at the time of the deflation after the Napoleonic Wars, we find Thomas Attwood insisting that 'so long as any number of honest industrious workmen in the kingdom are out of employment, supposing such deficiency of employment to be not local but general, I should think it the duty and certainly the interest of Government, to continue the depreciation of the currency until full employment is obtained and general prosperity'.[2] It is possible to find a host of 'unorthodox' writers both of the eighteenth and nineteenth centuries who took more or less the same line.

But the majority of economists of the classical tradition did not adopt this approach. It would be absurd to say that they were not interested in a high level of employment: the belief that, except among cranks, reference to the desirability of a state of something called 'full employment' is a post-Keynesian phenomenon rests on ignorance of the literature. But the classical outlook was apt to assume that there was a tendency to 'full employment' if other elements in the system were in a healthy state. It would have been readily admitted that monetary mismanagement might lead to unemployment. It is doubtful whether Hume's cautious formulations would have been overtly denied. But certainly the notion of making the state of employment the main criterion of monetary policy would have been rejected as involving a wrong focus, a focus liable to lead in the end to a state of inflation inimical to stability and growth.

[1] Law, *Money and Trade Considered* (1750) pp. 20–1.
[2] *Report from the Committee on Secrecy in the Bank of England Charter*, Parliamentary Papers (Commons) 1831–2, vi, Q 5758.

7. MONEY AND THE VOLUME OF TRADE

What then was the classical approach to this question? I think the answer must be that there was no overt approach. One could search the entire output of this school before, let us say, 1870, without finding anywhere a straight discussion of the connection between economic growth and the increase of the money supply. Needless to say, there is much discussion of the connection between prices and money supply. There is much discussion of the evil effects of instability in the value of paper money. But of the ideal requirements of money supply in a developing system there is no direct discussion.

This is not to say, however, that there are no implicit assumptions in this connection. On the contrary, propositions which we have already discussed have an intimate bearing on this matter. The emphasis, which is well-nigh universal, on the positive function of credit instruments in providing a substitute for the precious metals has just this aspect. It is true that this function is sometimes presented as involving chiefly a release of capital for productive investment. It is presented thus by both Smith and Ricardo. But there is another aspect which also emerges: if this substitute were not available there would be a restrictive pressure on prices with all the hampering influences that that would involve.

This comes out very clearly in Ricardo's exposition of his plan for an 'Economical and Secure Currency'. This is significant since of all the classical economists, save perhaps James Mill, Ricardo can be trusted everywhere to minimise the positive functions of money in regard to growth. 'Amongst the advantages of a paper over a metallic circulation', he suggests, 'may be reckoned, as not the least, the facility with which it may be altered in quantity as the wants of commerce and temporary circumstances may require, enabling the desirable object of keeping money at a uniform value to be, as far as it is otherwise practicable, securely and cheaply attained.' And he proceeds to justify this in terms of the inconvenience caused by having to circulate an increased volume of goods at lower prices. 'When the number of transactions increase in any country from increased opulence and industry . . . the economy in the use of money also continues unaltered— the value of money will rise on account of the increased use which will be made of it, unless the quantity be increased either by the addition of paper or by procuring bullion to be coined into money. There will be more commodities bought and sold but at lower prices. . . .' So that if an 'increase in the circulation were supplied by means of coin the value both of bullion and money would for a time at least, even after they had found their level, be higher than before; a circumstance which, though often unavoidable, is inconvenient, as it affects all former contracts.' If the increased need is met by paper, however, this need not occur.[1]

Thus, whether consciously or not, the classical writers who would have underwritten this view were in fact committed to an endorsement of the desirability, if 'inconvenience' was to be avoided, of some increase in the volume of money *pari passu* with increase in the volume of goods and transactions.

8. THE REAL BILLS DOCTRINE

But what degree of increase was desirable? On this no very clear agreement emerges.

Sir William Petty and Cantillon, among others, had suggested certain ideal proportions between the national product and the volume of money which clearly implied an increase in money when production increased.[2] But Adam Smith in *The Wealth of Nations* referring to such calculations expresses the view that this

[1] Ricardo, *Works*, vol. iv, pp. 55–8.
[2] For Sir William Petty's calculation see his *Quantulumcunque concerning Money*, Question 25, reprinted in *The Economic Writings of Sir William Petty*, ed. Hull (1899); for Cantillon's see his *Essai sur la Nature du Commerce*, pp. 131–49.

proportion 'is, perhaps, impossible to determine',[1] and in this he has been followed by most writers on this subject ever since. It was not until our own day that Cassel and some others have again suggested definite coefficients of increase.[2]

Was it then possible to regard the adaption of the volume of money to the needs of growth as self-regulating? Pretty obviously not if the circulation were purely metallic. Up to the end of the nineteenth century at least the discovery of gold and silver deposits and their exploration was an almost fortuitous business; and in any case the response of output to changes in value as indicated by movements of costs was likely to be so slow as to defy description in terms of conformity to any optimum. I do not know of any responsible economist who has ever made this claim, although I can believe that from time to time something like it may have come from the interests concerned.

Recourse to paper, however, has sometimes suggested other verdicts. At the time of the Restriction of Cash Payments, the claim was sometimes made by defenders of that system that if the Bank of England — or banks in general — would only adopt the practice of restricting its issues to the discounting of 'real bills' — bills, that is to say, arising in the course of 'genuine trade' as distinct from speculative operations — then all would be well and the volume of circulation would automatically adapt itself to the 'needs of trade'.

This doctrine, which could claim some respectability from hints to that effect in *The Wealth of Nations*, although these related only to convertible notes,[3] was of course based upon fallacy; and it was exposed as such — one would have thought once for all — by

[1] Smith, *op. cit.*, vol. i, p. 278.

[2] See Cassel, *Theory of Social Economy*, trans. McCabe (1923) vol. ii, p. 450, and Milton Friedman, *A Program for Monetary Stability* (New York, 1960) pp. 77–99.

[3] Smith, *op. cit.*, vol. i, p. 287. For a detailed history of the so-called 'real bills' doctrine see Lloyd Mints, *A History of Banking Theory in Great Britain and the United States* (Chicago, 1945) and F W Fetter, *The Development of British Monetary Orthodoxy* (Harvard, 1965).

Henry Thornton in a celebrated passage in his *Paper Credit* in which he showed that the volume of bills coming forward for discount was not an independent variable but itself depended upon the rate of discount in relation to the rate of anticipated profit. 'Any supposition that it would be safe to permit the bank paper to limit itself, because this would be to take the more *natural* course is therefore erroneous', he wrote. 'It implies that there is no occasion to advert to the rate of interest in consideration of which the bank paper is furnished, or to change that rate according to the circumstances of the country.'[1] Anyone who supposes that the idea of a cumulative price rise due to divergence between 'natural' and money rates of interest is a modern invention may be referred to the whole demonstration in which this passage occurs; it is perhaps still the most vivid analysis of this sort of thing in the whole range of the relevant literature.

The conclusiveness of Thornton's analysis, however, did not prevent a revival of the real bills doctrine in the more respectable context of the controversy with regard to the principles of the Bank Act of 1844.

The two leading opponents of these principles, Tooke and Fullarton, were anxious to refute the alleged necessity of any regulation of the note issue other than the obligation of convertibility; and to this end they sought to establish that so long as notes were issued on good security and were ultimately convertible there was no danger of over-issue.[2] This was the celebrated Principle of Reflux according to which any attempt to issue notes in excess of the needs of trade would be defeated by their immediate return; and although it differed from the position attacked by Thornton in that it was held only to apply to convertible paper, yet in the end, as Robert Torrens triumphantly showed, it depended upon the same fatal error of regarding the volume of applications for

[1] Henry Thornton, *Inquiry into the Nature and Effects of Paper Credit*, ed. Hayek (1939) p. 254.

[2] See Thomas Tooke, *Inquiry into a Currency Principle*, 2nd ed. (1844) p. 66; John Fullarton, *On the Regulation of Currencies* (1844) pp. 64–9.

loans and discounts as given independently of the terms upon which such facilities were offered.[1]

9. THE PRICE LEVEL AND DEVELOPMENT

The idea of a self-regulating mechanism directly responsible to the needs of trade, either with inconvertible paper or as a supplement to a metallic base, was clearly a false scent. But it was far on in the nineteenth century before there was much overt discussion of the degree of increase desirable even in an ideal closed system, let alone in a world of different moneys and different mechanisms of monetary supply. After the Return to Cash Payments in Great Britain with its intense deflationary pressures, so oddly minimised by the main classical economists, the intellectual energies of members of this school were chiefly preoccupied in this respect either with a rather wooden defence of metallic standards in general against paper heretics,[2] or with controversies concerning the regulation of bank issue with a view to avoiding financial crises. The gold discoveries of the late forties brought a period of rising prices whose 'powerfully beneficial effects' — to use Jevons' phrase[3] —on the general temper of economic activity did not escape notice. But it was not until the tailing off of these effects and the apprehensions of gold shortage caused by the abandonment, or prospective abandonment, of bimetallic standards, that speculation concerning the desirability of monetary policies or systems designed to offset such shortage became at all widespread.

[1] Torrens, *The Principles and Practical Operation of Sir Robert Peel's Act of 1844 Explained and Defended*, 3rd ed. (1858) pp. 203–36, 313–24.

[2] See for instance the most uncharacteristically severe attack on the position of the Attwoods by J. S. Mill in his paper, 'The Currency Juggle', reprinted in *Essays on Economics and Society*, pp. 181–93.

[3] W. S. Jevons, *A Serious Fall in the Value of Gold and its Effects* (1863) p. 62.

The great controversy regarding bimetallism, now almost forgotten, is the cradle of subsequent thought on the subject.

There are two aspects of this discussion which are especially deserving of notice from the point of view of this survey.

First it should be noted that throughout the immediate concern was focused on the value of money rather than on production or employment. The question under discussion was the question of the price level — should policy be directed to procure stable prices or prices gradually falling with productivity? It is true that the justification of policy — at any rate in part — was the effect on production. But this was not the immediate focus. As for the effects on employment, although these came into the discussion, it is safe to say that few of the participants would have adopted these as the ultimate criterion — not because they were indifferent to the ups and downs of employment but because they thought that these had a habit of adapting themselves to more fundamental influences and also, I am bound to add, because they would have thought, if it had been put to them, that exclusive concern with employment to the disregard of the value of money was likely to lead to bad effects both on production and distribution.

The second point to note about this discussion is its inconclusiveness as regards the final criteria of price movements. In so far as it was concerned with deliberate policy — and of course day-to-day policy as distinct from systems only gradually comes to the fore — there was no recommendation of price inflation. The benefits of an *unanticipated* rise in price levels and the accompanying profit inflation[1] were not unrecognised, although not without reserve. But the idea that an *announced* policy of continuous depreciation would have similar effects was something which has been reserved for the more naïve spirits of our own generation. After all it must be remembered that it was this period which saw the publication of Irving Fisher's *Appreciation*

[1] See for instance Keynes' (somewhat conjectural) attribution to this influence of the glories of Elizabethan literature in *A Treatise on Money*, (1930) vol. ii, p. 154.

and Interest — the classic demonstration that in this respect at least while you can fool some of the people some of the time, you cannot fool all the people all the time.

But on the relative merits of stability in the price of ultimate commodities or of stability in the prices of factor services there was no general agreement; and perhaps it is true to say that there is no agreement even at the present time. It would be beyond the scope of these lectures to trace in detail the course of the discussion from Marshall and Foxwell and Giffen in its early stages to Fisher and Keynes and Hawtrey in our own day. But perhaps it would be a fair generalisation to say that where distributive justice has been the main criterion, the argument has tended to favour the policy of prices falling with productivity on the ground that it would enable all participants in the economic nexus to benefit from the results of progress; and that where the effects on production have been the chief object in view, the policy of stable prices has been recommended on the ground of its gentle incentive to profit via the loosening of the burden of fixed debt. From the point of view of the theory of development, at any rate as regards the long period, therefore, perhaps the consensus can be regarded as being expressed by Marshall's cautious statement, 'I think the general interests of the country are best promoted by stationary prices.'[1]

10. FORCED SAVING

The theories discussed so far relate essentially to the role of increases in the supply of money in averting deflationary influences on prices or on providing some stimulus to increased activity. There is, however, another element in the classical analysis which relates to the possibility that in certain circumstances, increases in the money supply may result in increases in accumulation — the conception of 'forced saving'. This conception has made a

[1] Marshall, *Official Papers* (1926) p. 19.

good deal of noise in our own time. But in spite of the striking results of the researches of Professor Hayek [1] and Professor Viner,[2] it is doubtful whether the extent to which it was articulated in the classical literature is as yet fully appreciated. An examination of characteristic specimens therefore may form a fitting conclusion to this survey.

The first elaboration of this conception, it appears, was due to Jeremy Bentham who, in a manuscript eventually published by Bowring as part of the *Manual of Political Economy*, described at some length the nature and the possibilities of what he called 'forced frugality'. After indicating the possibility of additional saving being extracted from the citizens by taxation, he goes on to point out that 'the effect of forced frugality is also produced by the creation of paper money by the government or the suffering of the creation of paper money by individuals. In this case the effect is produced by a species of indirect taxation which has hitherto passed almost unnoticed.' If the additional money comes into the hands of those who use it as capital, then, 'all hands being fully employed', there is a tangible offset to the loss of real income on the part of the rest of the community. 'Here', he says, 'as in the above case of forced frugality' (through taxation) 'national wealth is increased at the expense of national comfort and national justice.'[3]

Bentham's *Manual* was not published until 1843, although the papers of which it was compounded, written more than forty years before, had some private circulation — as we know from Ricardo's correspondence. But in the published literature of the great period of monetary speculation during the suspension of cash payments there is abundant evidence of widespread understanding of the effect he described. Thus, in the course of a discussion of the effects of what he regarded as an undue expansion of credit

---

[1] F. A. Hayek, *Prices and Production* (2nd ed.) (1935) ch. 1, Profits, Interest and Investment (1939), pp. 183–97.

[2] J. Viner, *Studies in the Theory of International Trade* (1937) pp. 189–91.

[3] Bentham, *Works*, ed. Bowring (1843) vol. iii, pp. 44 *seq.*

— which incidentally pays full tribute to the possibility of initially favourable effects on employment — Henry Thornton is quite explicit on this point. 'It must be admitted', he says, 'that provided we assume an excessive issue of paper to lift, as it may for a time, the cost of goods though not the price of labour, some augmentation of stock will be the consequence; for the labourer, according to this supposition, may be forced by his necessity to consume fewer articles, though he may exercise the same industry'; and he goes on to allude to the possibility of 'a similar defalcation of the revenue of the unproductive members of the society'.[1]

Similar insights are to be found in the writings of authors whose views in other respects were completely disparate, such as Malthus, Lauderdale, Tooke, Torrens, Joplin and others.[2] Even Ricardo

---

[1] Thornton, *op. cit.*, ed. Hayek (1939) p. 239.

[2] Malthus, 'On Depreciation of paper Currency' *Edinburgh Review*, xvii (1811) p. 363. Earl of Lauderdale, *Further Considerations on the State of the Currency* (1812) pp. 96–7. Tooke, *Considerations on the State of the Currency*, 2nd ed. (1826) pp. 23–4. Torrens, *Essay on Money and Paper Currency* (1812) pp. 33–4. Joplin, *An Illustration of Mr. Joplin's Views on the Currency* (1825) pp. 28 ff.; *Views on the Currency* (1828) p. 146. Since Joplin's tracts are so rare and inaccessible, a quotation from this last may not be inappropriate: 'The notes of the bank thus issued always represent the savings of income, or answer the same purpose. If the issues of the bank are not increased by any loan it makes at interest, an equal amount of money must have been previously saved out of income, and paid into the bank, in which case, the party borrows the income previously saved; but if not, and the issues of the bank are increased by the loan, prices rise, and the party who has borrowed the money obtains value for it by depriving the holders of the money in previous circulation, of a proportionate power of purchasing commodities. An economy is thus created, though a forced economy, but it answers all the purpose of a voluntary one. It makes no difference to the party borrowing the money, whether the value he obtains for it, be previously and voluntarily saved, or saved by the power of consumption on the part of those who held the money in previous circulation, being limited. Hence, when the bank lends money at interest, it always lends the savings of income; it lends savings which either have been, or will be made.'

recognised the possibility, although he questioned the probability of its occurrence.[1]

Perhaps the most convincing evidence, however, of the general recognition of the possibility of forced saving, is its appearance in the works of John Stuart Mill, both in his *Essay on Profits, and Interest* and in the *Principles*. In the former there is a clear explanation of the process which he calls 'forced accumulation'.[2] In the latter a footnote, corrective of a bald statement in the text that credit involves a transfer rather than an increase of capital, runs as follows.[3] 'The circulating medium existing in a country at a given time, is partly employed in purchases for productive, and partly for unproductive consumption. According as a larger proportion of it is employed in the one way or in the other, the real capital of the country is greater or less. If, then, an addition were made to the circulating medium in the hands of unproductive consumers exclusively, a larger portion of the existing stock of commodities would be bought for unproductive consumption, and a smaller for productive, which state of things, while it lasted, would be equivalent to a diminution of capital; and on the contrary, if the addition made be to the portion of the circulating medium which is in the hands of producers, and destined for their business, a greater portion of the commodities in the country will for the present be employed as capital, and a less portion unproductively. Now an effect of this latter character naturally attends some extensions of credit, especially when taking place in the form of bank notes, or other instruments of exchange. The additional bank notes are, in ordinary course, first issued to producers or dealers, to be employed as capital: and though the stock of commodities in the country is no greater than before, yet as a greater share of that stock now comes by purchase into the hands of producers and dealers, to that extent what would have been unproductively consumed is applied to production, and there is a real increase of capital'.

[1] In the appendix to the fourth edition of *The High Price of Bullion*, reprinted in Ricardo, *Works*, vol. iii, p. 120–1.
[2] Mill, *Essays on Economics and Society*, p. 307.
[3] Mill, *Principles of Political Economy*, p. 528.

Thus it is clear that the conception which at one time was thought to have been introduced into economic analysis by modern writers such as Wicksell, von Mises and Robertson, in fact was known to wide circles of orthodox and unorthodox economists at a very much earlier period.

There is, however, one substantial difference between the earlier and later literature. We have seen already that Bentham's recognition of the possibility of 'forced frugality' of this kind was accompanied by marked disapprobation. It is safe to say that this was the attitude of most of the writers of that period. Thornton, for instance, commenting on the analysis already quoted, says baldly that saving brought about in this way 'will be attended with a proportionate hardship and injustice';[1] and John Stuart Mill, in the *Essay on Profits, and Interest*, roundly condemns the process of 'forced accumulation'. The fact that the depreciation of the currency is accompanied by the conversion of revenue into capital 'is no palliation of its iniquity. Though A might have spent his income unproductively, B ought not to be permitted to rob him of it because B will expend it on productive labour.'[2]

The modern verdict has not been so united or so unambiguous. It is true that followers of the main Austrian tradition, taking their tone from von Mises' masterly exposition, have tended to deprecate the forcing of saving. Some of them, including at one time the present author, although I think not von Mises himself, have doubted the eventual stability of all or nearly all such accumulations — thereby attributing to the impersonal working of the economic system a regard for equity which I am afraid there is no reason to suppose that it has.

But others have taken different views. Schumpeter, for instance, displayed no such scruple. In his conception of economic development, the process of forced saving through the credit system plays a quite central part: indeed, reading his famous monograph you would think that no accumulation worth speaking of could take place without it. And although Schumpeter always

---

[1] Thornton, *op. cit.*, p. 239.

[2] Mill, *Essays on Economics and Society*, p. 307.

insisted on his role of complete detachment, an observer noting only inevitable conditions and tendencies, I think it is not unjust to suspect that he would have regarded as pretty much of a fool anyone who did not accept this particular inevitability with some degree of private relish.   And certainly many of those who with self-indulgent frivolity have advised the unfortunate rulers of the so-called under-developed countries to go ahead with ambitious plans regardless of what happens to prices would probably not disagree with him.

But at this point we are clearly at the frontiers I have set myself. To me it is fairly clear that an *unexpected* fall in the value of money due to, or permitted by, an expansion of money supply may make some lasting addition to accumulation, if it does not get out of hand.   I am not clear that *expected* falls necessarily have this effect: moreover, on other grounds I should not be prepared to expect them to have results altogether favourable to growth.   But even if the general aim is some sort of stable money the fact must be faced that the ideal of neutral money which has fascinated many of us over the years rests probably on over-simplification.   As Robertson showed so elegantly, even a policy aiming at stable commodity prices may involve some forced saving.   The fact is that for the final solution, even on the highest level of abstraction, of the more intricate relations between money and growth, we must await further development of contemporary thought on the more dynamic aspects of the subject.   And there, you will remember, at the outset of these lectures I imposed a self-denying ordinance.

F

THE DESIRABILITY OF ECONOMIC DEVELOPMENT

I. INTRODUCTORY

I HAVE now touched, if only in a very superficial way, upon the main historical answers to what I have called the *why* — as distinct from the *how* — questions concerning economic development; questions relating to population, accumulation, education and knowledge, organisation and money; and at this point, therefore, the exposition could perhaps stop. Before quitting the subject, however, it may be interesting to survey — even more superficially than in the preceding lectures — various historically important attitudes on the desirability of economic development. Granted that development is possible, is it worthwhile? Or to put the question in a more reasonable manner — which has seldom been the case in the more conspicuous historic discussions — how has development to be valued at the margin in comparison with other ends? This plainly takes us far outside the bounds of analytical economics as it is usually, and in my judgment, properly, conceived. But, as I once said in an early essay which has given rise to much misunderstanding 'our methodological axioms involve no prohibition of outside interests.'[1] We may therefore proceed without bad conscience to investigate tentatively the history of the answers to one of the main questions of political economy in the wide, non-strictly scientific sense of that term.

[1] Robbins, *An Essay on the Nature and Significance of Economic Science*, 2nd ed. (1935) p. 150.

2. THE MEANING OF ECONOMIC DEVELOPMENT

Before doing this, however, it is necessary to say a few words about the general concept. It will be remembered that in the first lecture, having defined development in terms of increases in income per head or capacity to produce that income, I alluded to the possibility of conceptual complications but at that stage preferred to press on with my history. Now, however, awareness of these difficulties is very relevant to the subject matter of this chapter. It would be ill advised to discuss the various views of the desirability of economic development without at least some broad notion of the ambiguities in the central conception itself.

I have chosen to define economic development in terms of increasing real income per head or increasing potential to produce such income. Now if real income consisted in the availability of some homogeneous all-purpose stuff which could be used for food, clothing, shelter, decoration, defence and amusement, then the idea of increases or diminutions would be free from difficulty and measurement would be a very simple process. But this is not so. Real income is essentially *physically heterogeneous* — a flow of availability of different goods and services — bread, heating, transport, medical care, theatrical spectacles and so on. The idea of changes in the volume of such a collection is therefore necessarily much more complex; and measurement in any very exact sense may become virtually impossible. Without becoming over-involved in technicalities, let us remind ourselves of some of the more conspicuous difficulties.

The first arises in connection with changes in the relative availability of different constitutents of the same collection of goods. If, of a collection A, B and C, while A and B increase, C diminishes, what are we to say of the movement of the collection as a whole ? This is typical of a whole group of problems which, if we are thinking of them in relation to individuals with roughly the same tastes and the same money incomes, can, as we know, be reasonably well handled by the technique of index numbers. To take the limiting case of the real income of a single individual with a constant money income, if the prices of A and B fall while that of C increases, the answer to the question whether real income has risen or fallen will depend upon the relative weights to be attached in his system of valuations to the commodities in question.

But the comparative simplicity of this solution depends upon a multiplicity of assumptions which are not necessarily justified outside fairly narrow limits of time or space or social structure. Thus, to begin with the simplest complication, if we remove the assumption of roughly similar incomes, it is not difficult to see that changes in relative availabilities may involve increases of real income for some groups and diminutions for others. To take a very obvious example from the circumstances of our own day, the increases in manufacturing productivity which bring about increases in real income for wage-earners may at the same time involve such a shrinkage of the supply of domestic help as to bring about, because of the difference in weighting, a diminution of the real incomes of some professional people. Broad discussion of changes in income per head must assume away such sectional differences and proceed in terms of 'representative' men or families, a conception which clearly involves a judgment of value of a sort, although, if explicitly recognised as such, not likely to be seriously misleading.

But this is not all. Development is a process which must be conceived in relation to comparatively long periods. And in periods of such length the composition of the collections constituting real income is likely to change, not only in the relative availability of items of a given list, but also in the composition of the list itself. A representative list today in an area of western civilisation will involve many items not available at all a hundred years ago. It may also omit items which some at any rate would wish to be still available. And this is true not only of broad classes, it applies also perhaps in a higher degree to differences of quality within such classes; a radio set today is a radically different instrument from what went by the same name in the twenties. The indexes of growth in everyday use in contemporary discussion have notoriously a downward bias as regards improvement of quality. All this makes precision very difficult. We can imagine our representative man or family exposed to different collections available at different long intervals and we may imagine him (or them) capable of saying which he (or they) regarded as the greater. But we should find it much more difficult to suggest to him ways of saying how much greater.

Finally, and this is the most fundamental difficulty of all, comes the fact that the representative men of different periods may have different tastes and preferences. What is wealth in the valuation of one may be not-wealth in the valuations of another. The flesh of the pig is meat to some, prohibited poison to others. Such differences are very obvious if we are making comparisons of real incomes at different points of space; they are no less possible at different points of time. And this means that if comparisons of real income are not to be strictly relative to the valuations of one group, they must satisfy a double test. To say that income per head has increased from Period I to Period II, there must be evidence not only that the representative man of Period I would rate the income per head of Period II greater than that of Period I, but also that the representative man of Period II would make a similar rating.

Considerations of this sort inevitably suggest much doubt regarding measurements of real income per head between societies having widely different positions either in time or in space. And rightly so: even in regard to narrower differences, the apparent precision of contemporary statistics has a strong flavour of the naïve, if not of the bogus. Jacob Viner's famous wisecrack about those who are prepared to measure the immeasurable to three places of decimal is dead on target in this field.

Nevertheless it is important to preserve a sense of proportion in this connection. Because precision of measurement is impossible outside narrow limits and because judgments of change must always be related to valuations, it would be absurd to argue that no statements regarding development had any meaning whatever. The generalisations which have been reviewed in these lectures have been generalisations about the direction of movement rather than its exact pace or magnitude; and, although they seldom make plain all their implicit assumptions, it is clear enough that they can be formulated in a way which escapes the charge of independence of assumed valuations. Moreover, if we reflect on the versatility of a substantial proportion of productive agents and the fact that although men and communities differ somewhat in tastes and requirements they do not differ totally, we are entitled surely to conclude that there is not only meaning but practical importance in many of them. We may not be able to say quantitatively how much difference there is in income per head in North America today and in the time of the Red Indians. But it would be ridiculous to deny that we mean something which can be made intelligible when we say that there is a difference or that we are capable of explaining in general terms how that difference has come about.

Although, therefore, it may be said that much of the historical discussion of the desirability of development was not as self-conscious or as sophisticated as might have been desired or as we can make it, there is no reason to regard it as lacking in content or significance for action; and there is no reason why, being conscious of the difficulties, we should not discuss it in broad terms without pausing every minute to make all the necessary qualifications explicit.

3. THE GREEK PHILOSOPHERS

The attitude of the great Greek philosophers to this question was not merely indifferent, it was positively hostile. As Popper has argued — in my judgment conclusively — Plato and Aristotle, acutely sensitive to the strains of the developing Athenian economy, were against change.[1] They were against trade beyond a

[1] K. R. Popper, *The Open Society and its Enemies*, 2nd ed. (1952) vol. i, especially ch. 10.

certain very primitive level. They deprecated travel.[1] They were against the intrusion of foreigners — except as menial slaves or artisans. Dismayed by the disorder and changing values of the open society, they sought, in various degrees, to reimpose the habits and the hierarchical structure appropriate to unchanging conditions — Plato with fervid intensity, Aristotle with greater moderation. Born in an age when the city state was giving place to the more spacious organisation of the Hellenistic world, their gaze was fixed on the past. Plato's ideal state was an autarchy of a few thousand. The tutor of Alexander the Great considered only the politics of communities capable of being summoned into one place by the call of a trumpet. The open society was not one in which virtue or justice would flourish.

This hostility comes out very vividly in the conversation between Glaucon and Socrates in book II of the *Republic*. Socrates — or rather the Platonic Socrates — has laid down the mode of living in the ideal state and Glaucon objects that he has constructed a city of pigs.

[1] I cannot resist transcribing here Plato's prescriptions in *The Laws* regarding travel and foreign exchange. 'The law enjoins that no private man shall be allowed to possess gold and silver, but only coin for daily use, which is almost necessary in dealing with artisans, and for payment of all those hirelings whose labour he may require, whether slaves or immigrants. Wherefore our citizens, as we say, should have a coin passing current among themselves, but not accepted among the rest of mankind; with a view, however, to expeditions and journeys to other lands — for embassies, or for any other occasion which may arise of sending out a herald, the state must also possess a common Hellenic currency. If a private person is ever obliged to go abroad, let him have the consent of the archons and go; and if when he returns he has any foreign money remaining, let him give the surplus back to the treasury, and receive a corresponding sum in the local currency. And if he is discovered to appropriate it, let it be confiscated, and let him who knows and does not inform be subject to curse and dishonour equally with him who brought the money, and also to a fine not less in amount than the foreign money which has been brought back.' *The Dialogues of Plato*, trans. Jowett 2nd ed. (1875) vol. v, pp. 313-14. I owe this mordant anticipation of the state of affairs in Great Britain in 1967 to a citation by Popper, *op. cit.*, vol. i, p. 298.

'But what would you have, Glaucon, I replied.

'Why, he said, you should give them the proprieties of life. People who are to be comfortable are accustomed to lie on sofas and dine off tables, and they should have sauces and sweets in the modern fashion.

'Yes, said I, now I understand: the question which you would have me consider is, not only how a state, but how a luxurious state is to be created; and possibly there is no harm in this, for in such a state we shall be more likely to see how justice and injustice grow up. *I am certainly of the opinion that the true and healthy constitution of the State is the one which I have described. But if you wish to see the State in a fever, I have no objection*' (my italics).[1]

There is no such explicit limitation in Aristotle. But the condemnation of retail trade beyond what is necessary to provide the needs of the household springs clearly from a similar outlook.[2]

4. PRIMITIVE CHRISTIANITY

The teaching of the New Testament was not based on an active hostility to development as was that of Plato and Aristotle. But it led to much the same negative attitude. True, the Christian was taught to render to Caesar the things that are Caesar's; he was not told not to pay taxes. But for himself the maxim was to 'take no thought for the morrow: for the morrow shall take thought for the things of itself.' The injunction to consider the lilies of the field which neither toil nor spin, may perhaps be considered as residing on the same plane of truth as the poet Blake's warning that

> 'He who binds to himself a joy
> Does the winged life destroy.
> But he who kisses the joy as it flies
> Lives in eternity's sunrise.'

[1] *Plato, op. cit.*, vol. iii, pp. 243–4.
[2] Aristotle, *Politics*, trs. Welldon (1901) pp. 21–26.

which it were absurd to tie down as a rule of economic activity. But the preceding command to 'Behold the fowls of the air: for they sow not, neither do they reap nor gather into barns',[1] together with the very positive prohibition of laying up treasure on earth, 'where moth and rust doth corrupt and thieves break in and steal', has surely a less equivocal significance. It is the archetypal principle of asceticism and the world-rejecting life; and as such exercised a dominating influence on Christian thought for at least a millennium. Christianity, in its primitive form, was definitely nay-saying in regard to life in this world in contrast to life in the next.

To get this attitude into proper perspective two historical circumstances need to be borne in mind. First that, at least at the beginning of the period, under the domination of Rome, the connection between the individual and the Imperial authority was so attenuated that thought of any connection between considerations of individual duty or preference and public policy was almost excluded — at any rate for members of a minority sector ; and at a later stage when the authority of the Empire had given way to the confusion of the Dark Ages, such a conception must have been even more remote. Second, and even more fundamental, it must be realised that the early Christians, from their Founder downwards, spoke and acted as if they believed that the End of the World and the Last Judgment was almost immediately at hand. Why worry about economic development and the diminution of the general poverty of the human race, if at any moment, in the twinkling of an eye, the elect would be with their Lord? Had they not the Divine assurance that, while 'of that day no man, no not the angels which are in heaven' had exact knowledge, 'Verily I say unto you, this generation shall not pass, till all these things be done.'?[2]

As the centuries wore on and these expectations were not fulfilled the attitude of the Church became less unworldly. Certainly the great pontiffs laid up for themselves quite considerable treasures upon earth with, as I hope we should all agree, immeasurable benefit to the advancement of art and learning both then and

[1] Matt. 6: 24–34. [2] Mark 13: 30.

G

thereafter. And although St Thomas Aquinas, in his *Summa*, has little to add to Aristotle on matters of trade and economic life generally, except an analytical blunder about fungibles which was all his own, by the time we come to the works of St Antonino, written at the crest of the commercial greatness of Florence, activities conducive to such greatness are not treated as intrinsically unworthy of the God-fearing man or, when conducted with proper regard to general morality, as a disqualification for the rewards of the blessed hereafter.[1] Henceforward although, from time to time, the world-denying impulse continues to manifest itself in the works of individual thinkers, it cannot be said to be a major principle of Christian social philosophy. It is sometimes said that, of all the Italian communities, the Papal States were the most poverty-stricken and ill-administered. But it has never been argued that this was due to a deliberate adoption of the precepts of the Sermon on the Mount.

5. MERCANTILISM

It was the rise of the nation state which gave the impulse to the conception of economic development as a desirable objective of policy. Under the Roman Empire the area of administration was so vast, under feudalism the concentration of power so feeble, that the idea of policies deliberately adopted to bring about or facilitate economic change cannot readily have suggested itself to the speculative intelligence. But the emergence of the national unit, with all that that has implied for the consolidation of the Curse of Babel and the perpetuation of international anarchy, did mean that there had emerged a definite focus for the consideration of policy. The conception of the State was by no means totalitarian; the monarch or the Senate was not the prime mover in everything that happened. But that state action — or reaction — could have a powerful effect on the activities of the citizens, either positively or negatively, became readily apparent. Discussion of what such action should

[1] See B. Jarrett, *St. Antonino and Mediaeval Economics* (1914) ch. vii.

be therefore became part and parcel of the texture of political and economic discussion.

Now there has been much learned discussion of what the ultimate aims of policy were actually conceived to be in this period of nation-building. According to one school of thought, of which Heckscher is by far the most distinguished representative, the policy of Mercantilism in this sense was essentially a policy of power; considerations of plenty were strictly subordinate.[1] But according to Professor Viner, this is not so. Power was certainly an objective. But so too was plenty. The objectives were multiple; any attempt to reduce them to one oversimplifies the picture to the point of falsification.[2] I confess that, on my reading of the literature, the Viner position seems much the more plausible.

But whatever the merits of this controversy, one thing is certain: the development of economic potential was involved as a desirable objective. Whether the ultimate aim was power or plenty, or a combination of both varying with circumstances, there would have been virtually unanimity on the necessity of developing the powers of production which would facilitate the achievement of these aims. Not possessing exact conceptions in this respect — not yet measuring economic development in terms of present income per head or power to supply future income — the detailed expressions of this view were necessarily vague. But there can be no doubt of the general attitude. 'Ceux qui sont appellez au gouvernement des États doyvent en avoir la gloire, l'augmentation et l'enrichissement pour leur principal but. . . .' This was the opening sentence of the first work to call itself by the name of our subject — the *Traicté de l'Oeconomie Politique* of Antoyne de Montchrétien (1615). And it is safe to say that the content of the whole body of mercantilist literature is inspired by the same aim. *England's Improvement by Land and Sea*, the title of Yarranton's work already referred to,

[1] Eli Heckscher, *Mercantilism* (1935) part II, Mercantilism as a System of Power.
[2] Jacob Viner, *Power versus Plenty as Objectives of Policy in the 17th and 18th Centuries*, reprinted in *The Long View and the Short: Studies in Economic Theory and Policy* (Glencoe, Illinois, 1958) pp. 278–305.

is symptomatic of the mood of all. The development of productive power, whether for purposes of political and military strength or of plenty — that is the policy; and no flicker of reserve suggests anything but enthusiastic approbation of the objective.

There is one reserve, however, which must be registered by the modern historian. In general the desirability of development assumed by these writers was in the interests of only part of the society, the ruling classes and the merchants. There is little suggestion of the humane spirit of Quesnay's maxim: *Pauvres paysans, pauvre royaume; pauvre royaume, pauvre roi.* The attitude of Adam Smith that 'what improves the circumstances of the greater part can never be regarded as an inconveniency to the whole' finds small place in the mercantilist literature. 'No society', he continues, 'can surely be flourishing or happy, of which the far greater part of the members are poor and miserable. It is but equity, besides, that they who feed, cloath and lodge the whole body of the people, should have such a share of the produce of their own labour as to be themselves tolerably well fed, cloathed and lodged.'[1] On the contrary, as may be discovered from the masterly analysis of Furniss in his *Position of the Laborer in a System of Nationalism*, any rise of wages above subsistence level was viewed with intense apprehension. As we have seen already, education for the masses was deprecated lest it should make unskilled labour scarce. Doubtless there were exceptions: some at any rate of the propounders of recipes for national prosperity might have been willing to allow some of it to spill over to the labouring classes. But this was not the general attitude. Abundance of labour might be welcomed as a sign of prosperity. But the increased bidding which would give labour some share was pretty generally deprecated.

6. HUME AND SMITH

The Mercantilist conception of development was essentially a conception of something which was brought about by policy.

[1] Smith, *The Wealth of Nations*, vol. i, p. 80.

Exports were favoured and imports discouraged in order to promote the prosperity induced by an inflow of the precious metals. Foreign goods were excluded in order to foster the rise of industries considered to be basic. Hence there was little overt discussion of the desirability of development *per se*: if you bend all your powers to the recommendation of certain measures *because* they produce certain results, you do not spend much time discussing the results themselves: you tend to take that for granted. The mercantilists recommended policies tending, as they thought, to power and plenty. It would not occur to them to reflect on whether power and plenty were worthwhile.

It was otherwise with their eventual successors. The great eighteenth-century social philosophers, while not denying essential functions to coercive government and acknowledging many instances in which positive state action was beneficial, were chiefly interested in broader questions. They postulated a framework of law and order. They recognised as among the duties of the sovereign 'that of erecting and maintaining certain public works and certain public institutions, which it can never be for the interest of any individual, or small number of individuals, to erect and maintain . . .'.[1] But their main interest was focused on the spontaneous elements in economic society — on the way in which the private interests of individuals or small groups of individuals guided by the impersonal mechanisms of the market achieved a more or less orderly system of social co-operation and some at least of the prerequisites of economic growth. They saw markets and the organisation of production arising, like language itself, without any act of conscious collective choice. They saw the main influences which bring about economic development operating without central initiative. And their thought was directed to analyse these processes and to investigate the modes in which they operated. Hence it was to be expected that in this tradition there should be a conscious attempt to evaluate the results and

[1] Ibid., vol. ii, p. 185. On the classical conception of the functions of the state, see Robbins, *The Theory of Economic Policy in English Classical Political Economy*, chaps. 1–3.

explicitly to face the question whether economic development was or was not worth while.   And in fact such attempts are to be found.

Of such evaluations by far the most explicit and systematic is to be found in the work of David Hume.   'Were the question proposed', he says in the essay *Of Money*, 'which of these modes of living, the simple or the refined, is the most advantageous to the state or public? I should without much scruple prefer the latter, in a view to politics at least.'[1]   And in the essays *Of Commerce* and *Of Refinement in the Arts* he gives reasons for this preference.

The first of these two essays is an attempted vindication of the effects of commerce on the power and happiness of states.   When men have 'quit the savage state where they live chiefly by hunting and fishing' the arts of agriculture employ *at first* the most numerous part of the society.   But 'time and experience improved so much these arts, that the land may easily maintain a much greater number of men than those who are immediately employed in its culture . . .'.   And 'If these superfluous hands apply themselves to the finer arts which are commonly denominated the arts of luxury, they add to the happiness of the state: since they afford to many the opportunity of receiving enjoyments with which they would otherwise be unacquainted.'[2]   In the ancient world, it is true, they were often employed for the purpose of increasing the military power of the state.   But this was 'contrary to the more natural and usual course of things'.   In modern times, the legislator is best advised 'to comply with the common bent of mankind and give it all the improvements of which it is susceptible'.   If he does this he will find that 'industry and arts and trade encrease the power of the sovereign as well as the happiness of the subjects'.[3]   Furthermore 'a kingdom, that has a large import and export, must abound more with industry, and that employed on delicacies and luxuries, than a kingdom which rests contented with its native commodities.   It is therefore more powerful, as well as richer and happier.'[4]

[1] Hume, *Writings on Economics*, p. 44.
[2] Ibid., pp. 5–6.   [3] Ibid., pp. 8 and 10.   [4] Ibid., p. 13.

The essay *Of Refinement in the Arts* drives home these arguments: 'To imagine that the gratifying of any sense, or the indulging of any delicacy in meat, drink or apparel, is itself a vice, can never enter into a head, that is not disordered by the frenzies of enthusiasm.[1] . . . Ages of refinement are both the happiest and the most virtuous.[2] . . . In times when industry and the arts flourish, men are kept in perpetual occupation, and enjoy, as their reward, the occupation itself, as well as those pleasures which are the fruit of their labour. The mind acquires new vigour: enlarges its powers and faculties; and by an assiduity in honest industry, both satisfies its natural appetites and prevents the growth of unnatural ones, which commonly spring up when nourished by ease and idleness.'[3]

Moreover, the advanced state of industrial art is probably an indispensable prerequisite to good government. 'Laws, order, police, discipline; these can never be carried to any degree of perfection, before human reason has refined itself by exercise, and by an application to the more vulgar arts, at least of commerce and manufacture. Can we expect that a government will be well modelled by a people who know not how to make a spinning wheel, or to employ a loom to advantage?'[4] It is perhaps not surprising that the wretched Jean-Jacques Rousseau, beset by all sorts of psychological atavisms, should have felt uneasy in Hume's company.

Adam Smith's thought on this question is less systematic and more incidental to his treatment of other topics. But it is not difficult to piece it together into a consistent whole; and it is important to do so since it sets the tone of most subsequent classical *obiter dicta*.

The belief that it is desirable that there should be development in the sense of an increase in income per head or power to produce such income is implicit in the whole intention of *The Wealth of Nations*. This becomes explicit in the introduction to book IV, where the objects of 'Political Economy, considered as a branch

---

[1] Ibid., p. 19.   [2] Ibid., p. 20.
[3] Ibid., p. 21.   [4] Ibid., p. 24.

of the science of a statesman or legislator' are stated to be: 'first, to provide a plentiful revenue or subsistence for the people, or more properly to enable them to provide such a revenue or subsistence for themselves; and secondly, to supply the state or commonwealth with a revenue sufficient for the public services'.[1] All this, however, may seem a little formal. A much more vivid exhibition of positive approbation of development in this sense is to be found in the famous peroration of the opening chapter of book I contrasting primitive and advanced conditions, which I have quoted already when discussing population and returns, or by the section, in the chapter on wages in the same book, contrasting the human condition in circumstances of advancement or stationariness or decline with its conclusion that 'the progressive state is in reality the cheerful and the hearty state to all the different orders of the society. The stationary is dull; the declining melancholy.'[2] No one who has read the account of stationariness in China, not to mention that of decline in Bengal, can entertain any doubt which way Smith's aspirations lay.

It might be thought perhaps that this conclusion was rendered doubtful by the existence of the well-known passage in the *Theory of Moral Sentiments* in which it is said that 'in ease of body and peace of mind all the different ranks of life are nearly upon a level and the beggar who suns himself by the side of the highway possesses that security which kings are fighting for'.[3] But this would be a mistake. Adam Smith was arguing, as many others, from Bentham downwards, were to argue after him,[4] that the distribution of happiness was not so unequal as the distribution of wealth — a proposition which certainly involves a number of quite unverifiable assumptions. But whether or not in the last analysis it will stand up to exact analysis, it does not involve repudiation of the view that, other things being equal, the beggar by the roadside would benefit from an increase of real income.

[1] Smith, *op. cit.* vol. i, p. 395.   [2] Ibid., p. 83.
[3] Smith, *Theory of Moral Sentiments*, 11th ed. (1808) p. 444.
[4] Bentham, *Works*, ed. Bowring (1843), vol. iv, Codification Proposal, p. 541.

How much less does it involve the belief that an exposition of the 'science of a statesman or legislator' in respect of the increase of wealth is an exposition of activities which, on any ultimate view of human happiness, are worthless.

This, however, is not to say that Adam Smith was blind to the possible dangers of economic development. In the lecture on *Education and The Growth of Knowledge*[1] I have quoted at length the passage in which he dwells upon the narrowing effect upon character of extreme specialisation — that this was not an afterthought but a central feature of his outlook is proved by the fact that very similar sentiments are to be found expressed with almost equal vividness in the student's notes of his much earlier *Lectures on Justice, Police, Revenue and Arms*.[2] But the point to note in this connection is that recognition of this danger was a ground for recommending measures to offset it rather than to reverse the main process. In Smith's system, the dangers of industrial specialisation called for correction by state-aided education. They did not call for abandonment of the advantages of the division of labour, the condition of 'the greatest improvement in the productive powers of labour, and the greater part of the skill, dexterity and judgment with which it is anywhere directed or applied . . .'.[3]

7. NINETEENTH-CENTURY CLASSICISM

It is safe to say that the attitude to economic development which is exhibited by Hume and Adam Smith became part and parcel of the general position of later classical economists. They desired development. They thought that it was conducive to human

---

[1] Above, pp. 77–8.
[2] Smith, *op. cit.*, pp. 256–7.
[3] Smith, *The Wealth of Nations*, vol. i, p. 5. On this aspect of Smith's thought, Dugald Stewart's comments in his *Biographical Memoirs of Adam Smith, of William Robertson and of Thomas Reid* (1811) pp. 84–7, are very relevant.

happiness. They framed their prescriptions of policy with this objective in mind.

It is true that growing sophistication and more rigorous thought led to a clearer recognition of the distinction between positive and normative propositions. Thus in his *Notes on Malthus* we find Ricardo, for instance, insisting on the limitations of analysis as such. 'It has been well said by M. Say that it is not the province of the Political Economist to advise — he is to tell you how to become rich, but he is not to tell you to prefer riches to indolence, or indolence to riches.'[1] But we also find him declaring that he hopes the stationary state is far distant;[2] and we know that the reason was that, following Adam Smith, he held that, when accumulation was still positive, it was possible that wages would be above subsistence level, so there was at least a chance that during that period the labouring classes, as he would have called them, would learn habits of prudence as regards multiplication which would keep them at that level. And this we know to have been a common aspiration, at least among the Benthamite members of the school.

The position of John Stuart Mill, however, calls for special elucidation. For, as I mentioned in the first lecture, he went out of his way to say that he could not 'regard the stationary state of capital and wealth with the unaffected aversion so generally manifested towards it by political economists of the old school'; and he urged that while the struggle to get on was 'perhaps a necessary stage in the progress of civilisation' it was 'not a kind of social perfection which philanthropists to come will feel any very eager desire to assist in realizing'. The best state for human nature, he contended, 'is that in which, while no one is poor, no one desires to be richer, nor has any reason to fear being thrust back, by the efforts of others to push themselves forward'.[3]

This is pretty strong stuff and it is strengthened still further when he goes on to say: 'I know not why it should be a matter of congratulation that persons who are already richer than any one need be, should have doubled their means of consuming things

---

[1] Ricardo, *Works*, vol. ii, p. 338.   [2] Ibid., vol. i, p. 109.
[3] Mill, *Principles of Political Economy*, pp. 753–4.

which give little or no pleasure except as representative of wealth; or that number of individuals should pass over every year, from the middle classes into a richer class, or from the class of the occupied rich to that of the unoccupied. It is only in the backward countries of the world that increased production is still an important object: in those most advanced, what is economically needed is a better distribution, of which one indispensable means is a stricter restraint on population.'[1]

In the very next paragraph, however, Mill indicates the characteristics of the stationary state he would favour: 'a well paid and affluent body of labourers; no enormous fortunes, except what were earned and accumulated during a single lifetime; but a much larger body of persons than at present, not only exempt from the coarser toils, but with sufficient leisure, both physical and mental, from mechanical details, to cultivate freely the graces of life, and afford examples of them to the classes less favourably circumstanced for their growth.' Mill lived before the days of national income accounting and was obviously unaware of the fractional extent to which even completely egalitarian distribution would have led even the citizens of the most advanced communities towards this goal. Quantitatively considered, his utopia was still far distant. If he had realised that, there can really be little doubt what his attitude to further development would have been.

For there are two features of this chapter which deserve underlining if its intention and purport are not to be seriously misconceived. Firstly Mill's stationary state is, to use his words, a 'stationary state *of capital and wealth*' (my italics); it is not stationary as regards technique. He goes out of his way to emphasise the fact that a stationary condition of capital need not imply a stationary state of improvement, even of the industrial arts. But, and this is the second feature needing emphasis, the fundamental desideratum is restraint of population. It is possible that Mill underestimated the influences making eventually for increasing returns with populations larger than those of his day. But there can be no doubt that the main influence determining his attitude

[1] Ibid., p. 755.

to the prospect of stationariness was his burning conviction of the desirability of restraint on multiplication, not only in the interest of real income per head but also for the preservation of the non-pecuniary amenities of the countryside. It is in this chapter that there occurs his memorable outburst: 'Hitherto it is questionable if all the mechanical inventions yet made have lightened the day's toil of any human being. They have enabled a greater population to live the same life of drudgery and imprisonment, and an increased number of manufacturers and others to make fortunes. . . . they have not yet begun to effect those great changes in human destiny, which it is in their nature and in their futurity to accomplish.'[1]

These are not the sentiments of one who is opposed to development in the sense of an increase in income per head.

But while, therefore, we may regard the general classical tradition as favourable to development in this sense, it is important to make explicit the nature of this attitude. It was not an attitude which made growth the be-all and end-all of all activity and policy; we have had to wait to our own day for this frame of mind. It is to be remembered that *The Wealth of Nations* itself was part of a course in which he taught, to use the words of one of his pupils,[2] not only 'the principles of expediency' but also those 'of morality and justice'. One has only to remember his insistence, already cited, on the necessity of counteracting by education the unfortunate effects on character of industrial specialisation, to realise that his was not a support of economic development no matter what it cost in other connections; and we know that his attitude in this respect was shared by his followers in the nineteenth-century classical tradition. It is clear that the members of this school would not have favoured growth at the expense of intelligence or health.

To me at least it is equally clear that they would not have favoured growth at the expense of freedom. Since, with the

[1] Ibid., pp. 756–7.
[2] John Millar, quoted by Dugald Stewart in *Biographical Memoirs* (1811) pp. 14–15.

possible exception of John Stuart Mill, the nineteenth-century classical economists probably all regarded socialism in any possible form as productively inefficient, they did not confront this question explicitly.[1] If they had been asked whether they would prefer rapid growth under collectivism or less rapid growth under freer conditions, they would have replied that the choice did not arise, since growth would be less rapid under collectivism. But in this respect at least Mill can be regarded as a test case. He did not regard the institutions of private enterprise as necessarily the last word in social organisation; and on the strength of belief in the prospects of co-operative associations of workers, he called himself a socialist and entertained mild hopes of productive efficiency under such a regime. But the strength of his denunciation of state collectivism makes it clear that even if he had thought this to be more technically efficient than private enterprise, he would have rejected it on account of what he believed to be its menace to liberty: 'If the roads and railways, the banks, the insurance offices, the great joint stock companies, the universities, and the public charities were all of them branches of the government; if in addition, the municipal corporations and local boards, with all that now devolves on them, became departments of the central administration: if the employees of all these different enterprises were appointed and paid by the government and looked to the government for every rise in life: not all the freedom of the press and popular constitutions of the legislature would make this or any other country free otherwise than in name. *And the evil would be the greater, the more efficiently and scientifically the administrative machinery was constructed — the more skilful the arrangements for obtaining the best qualified hands and heads with which to work it*' (my italics).[2]

It should not be inferred from this that Mill was opposed to all paternalistic arrangements in all circumstances. His approval of 'an Akbar or a Charlemagne' for communities yet incapable 'of

[1] See my *Theory of Economic Policy in English Classical Political Economy* (1952) ch. iv and v, for a detailed examination of this question.

[2] Mill, *On Liberty* (1859) pp. 198–9.

being improved by free and equal discussion'[1] is evidence enough of that. But it is clear enough that for more advanced communities, he held liberty to be an objective even more important than growth. And I have no doubt that this would have been the attitude of his classical contemporaries if they had thought that the question really presented itself.

8. THE MARGINAL REVOLUTION

As we saw in the first lecture, the so-called Marginal Revolution contributed little directly to the analysis of development; and it would not be untrue to say the same of the discussion of the desirability thereof. Sidgwick and Marshall, who may be taken as representative of a neo-classical tradition which incorporated marginal techniques without rejecting the classical framework, may be judged to have had much the same attitude of cautious approval as their classical forebears. But the analytical focus of the 'revolutionaries', Jevons, Menger and Walras and their followers, was on matters other than growth or the movement of aggregates of production, and it was only natural therefore that appraisal of the social utility thereof does not figure large in their works.

Nevertheless, their innovations in analysis did contribute an invaluable technique to the rational discussion of this problem — the marginal method itself. The discovery that rational valuation relates to units of a given supply and not directly to the total supply itself, not only solved once and for all the famous paradox of value — the apparent superiority of the value of water to that of diamonds — it also suggested the appropriate form of any rational discussion of the relative valuation of alternative social ends. No one who has grasped the significance of the marginal approach is ever likely to wish to discuss such problems on an all-or-nothing basis — do we prefer growth, just like that, to its absence, also just

[1] Ibid. (1859) p. 23.

like that? In most conceivable situations it is a question of choice at the margin; what is our valuation of increments of growth in terms of the units of leisure or postponement of present real income which they involve? What extra percentage of the present national income should we be prepared to sacrifice for a unit increase in the growth rate? What degree of liquidation of the peasantry is worth a given increase in heavy industry? No doubt estimates of this sort involve all sorts of arbitrary valuations — the comparability at assumed ratios of the satisfactions of individuals, individuals now alive and individuals assumed to be born in the future — and social decisions of this sort are not in this respect on all-fours with the decisions of the private individual allocating his or her own income. But the approach via the comparison of more or less development at the expense of less or more achievement of other ends is an immeasurable improvement on the loose habit of comparison of all of one thing or all of the other. It is more realistic in regard to practical action. It is more rational in relation to the almost inevitably complex system of individual or social ends.

9. ANTIGROWTH ATTITUDES

It will be readily agreed that at the present day, in the value systems of large numbers of our contemporaries, the marginal estimation of development in terms of other alternatives has not been low. Indeed with many it has been so high as apparently almost automatically to exclude consideration of most other alternatives. In much contemporary discussion, growth seems to have become the be-all and the end-all of policy. Crude comparisons of crude index numbers have taken the place of more sophisticated considerations of policy. In some cases even cruder indices provide the guiding light: whatever their suitability, the output of steel, the possession of a refinery or an automobile assembly plant — psychological prestige symbols — are taken as appropriate

measures of economic progress. It is safe to say that those thinkers
of a former day who spoke well of development and sought to
explain the complex conditions under which it takes place would
be surprised at their spiritual progeny.

Brash fashions of this sort are apt to breed some reaction, and
so it has been in the present instance. Before concluding, therefore, it may be as well to take account of certain attitudes which
have developed in recent years in positive opposition to economic
development as we have known it.

There is no need in this context to take account of the nineteenth-century manifestations of this sort, the tirades against almost
everything by men such as Ruskin and Carlyle. For these were
mere denunciation with hardly a pretence of attempting to understand what was being discussed. Ruskin wrote some of the loveliest
prose in the English language in the earlier chapters of *Praeterita*;
and the catalogue of the Tintorettos in the Scuola della Rocca in
The Stones of Venice is something for which all men of sensibility
must hold him in gratitude. But we are really not obliged to take
seriously the social and economic thought of one who could
denounce Adam Smith as 'the half-bred and half-witted Scotchman
who taught the "deliberate blasphemy" — 'thou shalt hate the
Lord thy God, damn His laws and covet thy neighbour's goods.'[1]
This is the voice, not of candid reason and persuasion, but of
self-induced hysteria. Nor need we pay any more attention to the
eulogist of Frederick the Great, the author of the *Nigger Question*,
who stood opposite the Rothschild house at Hyde Park Corner
gloating on the torturing of the Jews in the Middle Ages.[2] We
know the type too well.

In recent years, however, there have developed critical appraisals
of the results of recent development by men better acquainted
with the nature of the economic system and the techniques with
which it may be analysed. Of these, at once the subtlest and the
most forceful is Dr E. J. Mishan's *The Costs of Economic Growth*

[1] John Ruskin, *Fors Clavigera*, new ed. (1896) vol. iii, pp. 259–60, 456.
[2] J. A. Froude, *Thomas Carlyle: A History of his Life in London* (1884)
vol. ii, p. 449.

(1967); and it will therefore serve the purpose of this analysis and make explicit the implicit basis of my own appraisals in this lecture if I select it for more detailed comment.

Dr Mishan's book is a powerful denunciation not only of economic growth but of the prevalent spirit of the age; and there can be little doubt that a certain fundamental pessimism and sensitivity colours his verdicts on some developments which others would value differently. But if we ignore his obvious dislike of change as such and his distaste for large political units, at some points almost reminiscent of the ancient Greek philosophers, there is a solid core of indictment which must be taken very seriously.

His main analysis falls within the framework of the concept of external diseconomies. This concept, of course, is not new. It is, so to speak, the algebraic counterpart of that concept of external economies which we have met before in the lecture on Organisation and Policy; and it has been developed in our own age by Pigou and Professor Meade, among others.[1] But no one has given it so wide a coverage or used it with such argumentative force as Dr Mishan. Whether he commands agreement or not, the reader will be lacking indeed in sensitivity if he does not appreciate the strength of his denunciation of the miseries of road congestion, the spoliation of the countryside, the destruction of peace and quiet by aircraft and other such-like evils. There is some of the best polemical writing of the age in this slender book.

Nevertheless, in attributing these evils to economic growth as such, Dr Mishan seems to me to have established a faulty perspective. Most of the subjects of his complaints seem to be attributed to circumstances not necessarily connected with economic development, and indeed, highly desirable to avoid if that process is to be salutary.

The first is pressure of population. Few, I imagine, would differ from Dr Mishan in deploring the by-products of this

---

[1] I may perhaps be permitted to refer to my own treatment of the subject in my, *The Economic Problem in Peace and War* (1947) pp. 18–22.

tendency. The prospect, which is a real one, of a southern England which is one vast suburb must fill any healthy mind with horror. But growth of population in already well-populated areas is not necessarily connected with growth of income per head. Certainly it was not conceived that way by the nineteenth-century exponents of the benefits of development. And, in my judgment at least, many if not all of the most conspicuous evils which Dr Mishan denounces would tend to disappear if the increase of numbers were to cease, still more if there were some tendency to reduction.

Secondly, comes what may be called *laissez-faire* as regards environment. Even given population growth, there is little to be said in vindication of the wholesale neglect of amenity in the urban developments of this century. The ruin of the pleasant landscapes of the Home Counties amid which I grew up as a boy is not the work of the Victorian era; it has taken place in our times. The layout of development is something which should not be left to individual initiative. The heritage of amenity of artificial landscape and urban squares comes from an age when the distribution of property was such that to leave it in the hands of large property owners did not necessarily lead to bad results — often very much the contrary, indeed. But in the present more egalitarian age, to do so is disastrous; the aggregate result of individual decisions is often something which the individuals responsible would themselves never have wished. Except as a result of pure flukes, only some collective control of the geographical development can produce environments which are individually acceptable. It has been neglect of this obvious consideration which has made an odious shambles and a spiritual desert of so much town development today.

But both these evils, population pressure and the results of *laissez-faire* on the environment, are evils which can be remedied without forgoing the benefits of economic development. Population growth has probably reached a stage in many parts of the world at which it should be deprecated on the narrow grounds of effects on production per head apart from the wider, but equally valid, grounds of effects on general amenity. It is indeed a movement which must be halted if the conditions of life on this planet are to remain remotely tolerable. As for the external dis-economies of uncontrolled geographical development, they should plainly be regarded as calling for corrective action equally with other by-products of development which give rise to adverse neighbourhood effects. There is certainly nothing in the classical or neo-classical tradition as regards the desirability of development, from Hume and Adam Smith onwards, which would contradict this verdict.

But this does not involve the rejection of growth as such: quite the contrary, indeed. It is true that control of the physical layout costs money — that it involves the use of real resources which otherwise might have increased the rate of development as measured by crude indices of production per head. Rimbaud's march towards the splendid towns of the future is not to be achieved without sacrifice in this sense. But the greater the growth of productivity in the non-amenity sphere, the more easily can this sacrifice be afforded. It has always been the areas of relatively great productive power which have produced the great cultures. There is nothing in history which would warrant the belief that the arts of civilisation are associated with poverty in this respect. On the contrary, all that we know of the poor periods and the poor areas sustains the description of the life therein as nasty, mean, brutish and short. It may be freely conceded that riches in the sense of high productive power are no guarantee of the emergence of worthwhile cultures. But the fact remains that, without such potentialities, worthwhile cultures are unlikely to be forthcoming.

A valid advocacy of economic development is surely one which will take all these considerations in its stride. It will not deny the dangers of growth in the crude sense. It will positively support measures to offset them. But it will recognise too that the growth of productive power per head has been one of the main influences emancipating us from the beastliness and squalor of primitive conditions and is moreover one of the main hopes for further progress, not merely in the material, but also in the spiritual sphere. It will urge therefore that to decry economic development in general in order to prevent some of its otherwise preventible disagreeable by-products is to risk destroying the basis on which ultimately both amenity and cultural achievement depend.

SELECT INDEX OF PROPER NAMES

177

attention of his general theory conditioned by the circumstances of the thirties, p. 20 ; his praise of Malthus on under-consumption, p. 59 ; his pessimistic appraisal of the schedule of the marginal efficiency of capital and its effect on his contemporaries, pp. 66–69 ; his reference to the underworlds of monetary theory cited, p. 136 ; on gold inflation and the glories of Elizabethan literature, p. 143

KNIGHT, CHARLES. His *Results of Machinery* a veritable psalm to the benefits of invention, p. 90

LANGE, O. His discussion of the price system under collectivism cited, p. 119

LARDNER. His treatment of railways outside the main classical tradition, pp. 109–110

LAUDERDALE, THE EARL OF. His under-consumption theory, pp. 57, 58 ; as a stagnationist, p. 67

LAVINGTON. His *Trade Cycle* in the tradition of J. S. Mill's essay *On the Influence of Consumption on Production*, p. 66

LAW, JOHN. His authoritative statement of the inconveniences of barter, p. 121 ; on the advantages of abundance of money, p. 131 ; the *débâcle* of his plans, p. 131 ; argues the dependence of trade and employment on the volume of money, pp. 136–137

LERNER, PROFESSOR A. His discussion of the price system under collectivism cited, p. 119

LETICHE, J. M. His edition of Gervaise cited, p. 125

LIST, F. His argument for the promotion of productive power, p. 116

LOCKE. Influence on the classical tradition of his rejection of the belief in innate ideas, p. 71

LONDON POLITICAL ECONOMY CLUB. The comparative neglect by its members of public utilities and railways, p. 109

LUTHER. His enthusiastic philoprogenitiveness, p. 23

McCULLOCH, J. R. His emphasis on the productivity of educational investment, p. 75 ; cited by Cannan as neglecting the importance of knowledge, p. 83 ; his review of Babbage a disproof of this accusation, pp. 91–92 ; his fulminations against the principle of limited liability, p. 107

MACHIAVELLI. An anticipator of Malthus, p. 26

MALTHUS, T. R. The place in the classical system of his theorems regarding population and diminishing returns in agriculture, p. 12 ; increasing population a sign of the happiness and prosperity of a state, p. 24 ; the first version of his Population Theory, pp. 28–31 ; his second thought, pp. 31–33 ; his rejection of contraception, pp. 31–32 ; his comparison between ratios of potential food and population increase and the idea of diminishing returns, pp. 34–35 ; his under-consumption theory, pp. 58–60 ; his repudiation of the assumption of hoarding, p. 60 ; as a stagnationist, p. 67 ; on forced saving cited, p. 146

MANDEVILLE, B. His *Fable of the Bees* and under-consumption, pp. 45–46 ; his hostility to education of the working classes, p. 74

MARSHALL, A. His sense of continuity in the evolution of thought, p. 14 ; his emphasis on the interdependence within the economic universe, p. 14 ; the emphasis upon growth in his *Principles*, pp. 16–18 ; his objection to J. B. Clark's division between static and dynamic analysis, p. 17 ; his interpretation of Malthus's arithmetical ratio of food increase, p. 34 ; his

52 ; on the effective desire of accumulation, pp. 52, 53 ; exhibits liquidity preference as a function of the rate of return on investment, p. 53 ; his profound eulogy of invention, p. 89 ; his argument for the protection of infant industry, pp. 113–114

RAMSEY, FRANK. His state of 'Bliss' said to arrive earlier under collectivism, p. 119

RICARDO, DAVID. Conceives political economy as preoccupied with distribution, p. 11 ; his overt fear of the stationary state, pp. 13, 166 ; less realistic, more logical than Malthus, p. 60 ; his concern for value and distribution renders him immune from Cannan's structures regarding the neglect of knowledge, pp. 90–91 ; his focus on narrower problems not to be taken to imply rejection of the Smithian system of natural liberty, p. 102 ; on credit as a substitute for money, pp. 127–128 ; on the advantages of elasticity of credit, pp. 128–129 ; argues the advantage of paper over metal in terms of the facility of adaptation of increases in the volume of trade, pp. 138–139 ; his recognition of the possibility of forced saving, pp. 146–147

RIST, CHARLES. His comparison of Law and Cantillon cited, p. 132

ROBBINS, L. His insistence that the recognition of the distinction between 'is' and 'ought' imposes no limitation on a catholicity of interests, p. 150 ; his *Theory of Economic Policy in English Classical Political Economy* cited, p. 161 ; his examination of the attitude of classical economist to collectivism cited, p. 169 ; his treatment of external dis-economies cited, p. 173

ROBERTSON, DENNIS. His tentative view of the positive function of fluctuations, pp. 18, 118 ; his frequent reference to Marshall and the trade cycle, pp. 65–66 ; his reintroduction of the conception of forced saving into modern analysis, p. 148

ROSENBERG, NATHAN. His refutation of allegations of contradictions in Adam Smith on the division of labour, p. 78

ROUSSEAU, JEAN JACQUES. His natural antipathy to the civilised outlook of David Hume, p. 163

RUSKIN, JOHN. His intemperate abuse of Adam Smith, p. 172

SAINT-SIMON. His estimate of the contributions of science, p. 88 ; contrasts the effects of the disappearance of monarchs and business men, p. 103

SAY, J. B. His division of the subject matter of political economy, p. 11 ; the *Loi des Débouches*, p. 55 ; the assumptions of his 'Law' examined by J. S. Mill, pp. 63–64 ; his objection to the Smithian conception of profits, p. 104

SCHMOLLER, G. His conception of Mercantilism, p. 5

SCHUMPETER, J. His theory of economic development, p. 16 ; his conception of fluctuation as a positive contribution to growth, p. 18 ; his distinction between innovation and routine management probably unacceptable to the classical school, p. 103 ; his heroic innovators descended from Clark and Walras, p. 104 ; the central position of forced saving in his conception of economic development, pp. 148–149

SCHWARTZ, PEDRO. On Mill's intervention in the water supply controversy, p. 110

SENIOR, NASSAU. Three out of four of his 'Elementary Propositions focussed on the theory of development, p. 12 ; his correspondence with Malthus cited, p. 32 ; his formulation of the idea of diminishing returns in agriculture and increasing returns in manufacture, p. 36 ; his failure to integrate sufficiently the idea of the division of labour and increasing returns, p. 39 ;